Dedicated to:

Game Warden-Conservation Officers
Rance Hill & George Bruso
(Two super people to have worked with)

&

Brothers Butch and Jack who made for some
great stories and later became my friends.

Phil.1:6

God save our gold

Printed by:
A & J Printing
P.O. Box 518
Nixa, MO 65714

Published by: J.A.W.'s Publishing

Order From:
John A. Walker
530 Alger Ave.
Manistique, MI 49854
Phone: 906-341-2082
E-mail: jawspub@juno.com

Library of Congress Cataloging-In-Publication Data
Walker, John A.

ISBN 0-9639798-6-8

3rd Printing

John A. Walker writes for:
Manistique Pioneer Tribune
212 Walnut St.
Manistique, MI 49854
Phone: 906-341-5200

These stories are written to show the humorous side of working as a Game Warden - living in Michigan U.P. They are not meant to offend anyone and are just the writers version of the stories as he heard or saw them. No names are used in the stories without prior approval.

Dedication

I guess one thing you would have to admit if you knew both of these old game warden is the fact that they were about as different as day and night.

Rance, was just what you would expect from an old X-Marine. If you could ever call someone a game warden's-game warden it would be Rance Hill. His attitude was just what you could understand with his Marine training. It was gung-ho and full speed ahead. His attitude toward the poachers never seemed to let up a bit even when he was our District Supervisor.

One of the main things that a working game warden liked about Rance was the fact if something ever came up he was there in your corner fighting for you. Rance did not really care whom he had to take on to protect his men under him, if his men were in the middle of something, Rance was right there with them.

The job as a game warden was the best job you could have, you wore the uniform with pride, and you were expected to perform your job, as it should be done, and Rance saw that you did.

Now George was a totally different personality than Rance was, but still the kind of Game warden that was out there to help those officers working out in the field. I can recall all the times when an officer in the field needed something from Lansing, George would always come through and see that you got it. To me he was always a serious type officer that wanted to provide a service for others.

As I sit here, many years after George has retired, I think of the job he does for all of us that have retired. George sees that we keep in touch through the Retirees News Letter. He now collects and types up all the little news worthy information of who did what, what crew held a get together, and how the families of former DNR employees are doing.

I know from the projects that I have undertaken since I retired that this is no easy task. By doing my weekly newspaper article then writing and self-publishing my books, I know the time and work that goes into collecting and getting all this news together. So this is my way of saying "Thanks" to George for keeping us all well informed about all our "Family" of retirees.

In order to have a good game warden story you have to have both the chaser and the chasee. In some of my best stories the chasees were a set of brothers. You would have to read the stories in my first couple of books to read about these two brothers. This is what I wrote after one of the brothers died of cancer.

We have always had a joke at coffee. The one positive thing about a weekly newspaper is you can check the obituaries and if you are not in it you can have another week to go to coffee. As you know, I have been on the road for a month going to Florida. Upon coming back home I was out at camp for a couple of days. Thursday night after returning home wifee asks me if I had read the obituaries? I had not so she told me what was in it.

You see it was twenty-five years ago this week that I came to Manistique. When I came here there was this older officer that lived here and showed me around. One thing I was soon to learn was that he called Tanery Road Death Valley. This was on account of who lived on this road. During my travels I came to learn about Butch and Jack. It seems that this older officer knew them rather well. I cannot ever remember meeting them until we crossed paths one night while I was working. The fire officer working with me knew who they were, but not me. The way things turned out we all laughed through the years about what took place.

I was also to hear some other tales that involved Butch and Jack. Man, could I get them going about some of the things I heard and what they would claim really happened. In fact not too long ago I got them going at coffee about the tale about what happened one spring where they claimed they were just some victims of being in the wrong place at the wrong time. They would both be talking at once trying to convince me that what I heard was not what really took place at all. I would just sit there and laugh as Butch would really get going and Jack would just be saying, "No lie John, that's really what happened."

In my books there are a good number of stories about this crew and some of their relatives. But sitting here typing this Fish Report, I can say that there have not been two people that this old game warden has had more fun with than Butch and Jack. You would have to get a set of my books to try and figure out which tales these two brothers starred in.

Butch always wanted a cut from my books and Jack could not believe that some of their adventures were helping youth from our town attend college. At the end of this month there will be another $1,000.00 in scholarships given out.

When I was sitting out at camp today I got to thinking that Jack has to be up there with a crossword puzzle or else that other goofy thing in the paper where you have to figure out what word should be in what spot. But I will tell you that once again coffee will not be the same as another one of the crew rides off to that perfect deer blind in the sky.

The Title & Cover

I guess one of the things that really amazed me was the fact that so many people that were caught out violating ran home to mother or their wife. Here is someone caught shining and shooting deer only when they appear in court they have mother with them. A forty, year old man bringing mom to court with him. I ask you is this normal?

I can still recall the day one of the locals that had been caught with illegal deer a number of times came up and told me his wife had just packed up and left him. I looked at him and said, "You have to be kidding me!" "Now, how many years has she been working to pay for all your fines and had to stay home alone while you did jail time. Is it any wonder she finally got fed up?"

He looked at me and said, "You know your right." You see for some people up here it is just a way of life.

The deer on the cover of this book is a pet buck of the man that owns the Deer Ranch over in St. Ignace. This man has a great time with his pets and they are almost like family to him.

Now if only I could come across his great grandpa out at my deer blind sometime. I would not be able to settle down enough to shoot at him, but I would sure like to see him sometime.

Index

Dedication
Index
Forwarned

<u>Chapter</u>

1- A Guy Thing 1-6

2- History of the DNR Air Force 7-8

3- The DNR Air Force 9-14

4- The Art of Getting Stuck 15-22

5- Dad, Tell The Truth Now 23-24

6- Little Quirks That Make Life Interesting 25-30

7- Some Short Stories 31-36

8- Rocky-My Best Friend-by Cathy Walker 37-38

9- Modern Math of the Millennium 39-44

10- Trees 45-50

11- Don't Be Fooled 51-54

12- Guardian Angels 55-57

13- Old Age 58-61

14- Emergency Landing 62-67

15- Friends? 68-73

16- Family 74-79

17- Great Minds 80-87

18- Life is Not Always Fair 88-93

19- Don't Tell Wifee 94-99

20- Tales About Wolves 100-105

21- A Yooper Vacation 106-111

22- Glossary 112-122

Forwarned

This book makes book number six in the "Tales From A Game Warden" series by Sergeant John A. Walker a retired Michigan Conservation Officer. When Officer Walker self-published his first book titled A Deer Gets Revenge he had no idea that he would be doing book number six, almost 40,000 books later. As Sergeant Walker tells it, "It is totally amazing how an unknown writer for a little Michigan Upper Peninsula newspaper can self-publish a series of books and sell this many of them."

These books of Sergeant Walkers are written just like his Grandpa Theiler used to sit around and tell his Grandkids stories back in the late forties and early fifties. It was back when story telling was really an art all it's own in the backwoods of Northern Wisconsin and Michigan's U.P.

Some twenty years ago Sergeant Walker started writing a weekly article for the local newspaper in the town where he lived. (The Manistique Pioneer Tribune) The newspaper article started out being a "Fish Report" for the local paper, but soon evolved into a story telling article. In fact Sergeant Walker now says that if to many of the articles now tell too much about fishing he starts too get complaints from his readers. Sometimes you just cannot win.

In talking about his series of books Sergeant Walker says if anything has helped sell his books it's the clean, family-style way the stories are told in these books. In the forewarned section of his first book he tells about his Mother using Fels-Naptha soap when her children used bad words and the fact he is still scared to use them fifty years later. Could it be that there are those out there that were just ready for books of this nature?

Sergeant Walker's five books already in print have sold all over the United States and been sold in six other countries. People of all ages and from every walk of life love these books. They are written with the backwoods flavor of his Grandfather telling stories to the grandchildren back in the late 40's and early 50's.

The scholarship fund started with the profits from the sales of Sergeant

Walker's books has help to raise more than $33,000.00 to help youth attend Christian Colleges. To date more than $12,000 has been given out in scholarships to students. It is Sergeant Walker's hope that someday the scholarship fund will be self-sufficient so it can continue on indefinitely.

The five books in the series "Tales From A Game Warden" covers the time that Sergeant Walker was growing up in the little town of Ontonagon in Michigan's Western Upper Peninsula. The tales tell about a lot of the family values he learned in this small town and the people he grew up with.

The books also have tales of the crazy things that happen to both the Game Wardens and those involved in hunting and fishing. It is the way Sergeant Walker has of telling the stories that makes them so interesting to so many people. There is no doubt you will learn to love these books as you learn about Sergeant Walker, his family, and those he worked with.

Map of Yooper Land

The U.P.
Upper Michigan

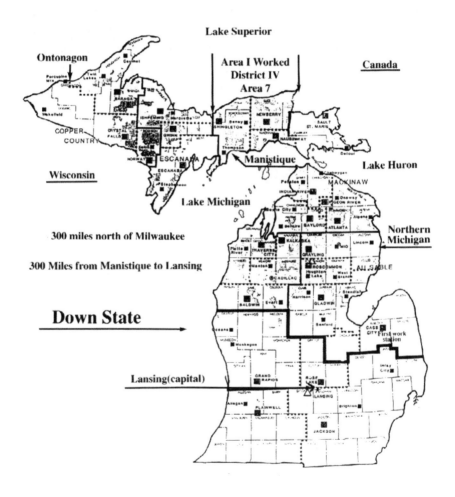

Chapter 1
Hunters at Their Finest

Well when you really stop to think about it you really have to be able to understand a Yooper by what he means not what he says. If on top of being a Yooper he is either a hunter or fisherman you really will need an interpreter to help you out. Here are a few cases where what he says is not always what he means.

"It's a guy thing."
Really means: "There is no rational thought pattern connected with it, and you have no chance of making any logical sense out of it." When nobody can make any normal sense out of what you are doing the week before deer season.

"Can I help you with dinner?"
Really means: "Why isn't dinner already on the table when I get home from hunting?" Of course there is no way anyone had any idea just when that would be.

"Uh huh", "Sure honey", or "yes, dear."
Really means: "Absolutely nothing!" It's a conditional response when a guy spends too much time out in the woods talking to himself or his dog.

"It would just take to long to explain."
Really means: "I have no idea how it works or why I even bought it, but it was a really good deal."

"I getting more exercise lately."
Really means: "There is not a remote for the TV up at camp."

"Shooting hours and/or daylight is almost here."
Really means: "Now I have a legitimate excuse to drive like a maniac on those icy, two-track roads to get to my favorite hunting spot on time."

"Take a break, honey, you're working too hard."

Really means: "I can't hear the TNN outdoors show over the sound of the vacuum cleaner."

"That's interesting, dear."
Really means: "Are you still talking, I could not hear you over the noise from the outdoor show."

"Honey, we don't need material things to prove our love."
Really means: "I forgot our anniversary again and spent my allowance on a new hunting video."

"That's women's work"
Really means: "It's a difficult, dirty, thankless, task and the only time I would even consider doing it is up at hunting camp."

"Oh, don't fuss. I just cut myself, it's no big deal."
Really means: "I have almost severed a limb cleaning my deer, but will gladly bleed to death before I admit I'm hurt."

"I do help around the house."
Really means: "There was a time (once) that I did pick up all my hunting magazines and gear that is laying around the house."

"Hey, I've my reasons for what I'm doing."
Really means: "I sure hope I can think of some reason pretty soon that will justify what has happened."

"I can't find it."
Really means: "My hunting/fishing gear that I haven't spotted since I last used it didn't fall into my outstretched hands, so I'm completely clueless as to what I did with it at the end of season."

"What did I do this time?"
Really means: "What did you catch me doing this time that there is no way a normal person could ever justify?"

"I heard you."
Really means: "I have no idea what you just said, and am hoping desper-

ately that I can fake it well enough so that you don't spend the next three days telling me I never listen to you anymore."

You look terrific!"
Really means: haven't we looked at enough stuff during the "payback" after deer season shopping trip to Green Bay?"

"I missed you."
Really means: "All my hunting clothes need washing, there is mud all over the kitchen floor, and the garage is a mess."

"We share the housework."
Really means: "I come home from hunting, make a mess and you clean it up."

"I'm not lost. I know exactly where I am."
Really means: "I'm lost! I have no idea where we are, but we haven't crossed US-2 or M-28 so we are still in the U.P. and there is no way I am ever going to admit it and ask directions."

....

A Suggestion?

While sitting in my deer blind, one day, I came up with a brilliant idea even for me. We all know that it cost big bucks for those of us that enjoy the outdoors. If you like to hunt and fish tons of money goes out for hunting and fishing supplies and gas to get back and forth. Now I figure that if you guys out there would just get wifee one of those coin operated washers and dryers like they have at a laundromat, you could collect all the money it would cost wifee to do the wash at home for hunting and fishing expenses. Now there are many advantages to this. Not only would you make a few bucks, but also the kids would not get so dirty all the time if it cost them for washing their clothes. Besides this would not affect most guys, because they would wear the same clothes at least two weeks between each wash. So think about it guys and order one of those coin operated washers and dryers for wifee for Christmas and it might go over a little better.

....

A Guy's Reaction

I think the DNR should take care their own problems before worrying about ours!! It seems this hunter took a load of sugar beets out and dumped them right in the yard at hunting camp. Now needless to say DNR protected deer never heard about the new baiting laws, or could care less about it. Not only did they come in and wreck his yard, they were eating those oversized sugar beets before he ever got to cut them into bite size morsels. Now how can a hunter be law abiding if the animals are not playing by the rules too? It could wear a guy out trying to chase the deer away from those oversized sugar beets day and night, twenty-four hours a day, with no sleep, what's a guy to do?

....

Anti-Harassment Laws For Hunters

I never thought I would see the day that a law was passed to protect us hunters from some of the things we have to put up with around the home.

We all know we have stalking laws and such to protect women from guys that go off the deep end. But! Now they seem to have passed a law to protect us guys so we are able to enjoy the right to our sporting activity free from unreasonable and deliberate interference! Could it be that it goes this far?

Your girl friend or wife had better watch out! We hunters now have the law on our side!

I really never thought I would see the day that they would pass a law and put it in black and white that a person's spouse can no longer get on his case about all the time spent hunting and fishing. Now, I'm not sure if this law goes as far as it should and covers the area where a guy throws his hunting gear all over the house and leaves it there for someone else to pick up.

See knowing some of those people that work down in the big house I'm not sure they understand a guy's right to place an old stinky pair of socks and rubber boots in front of the hot air vent in the living room so they will dry out over night. This is important if he is going to enjoy his rights, free from unreasonable and deliberate interference...cold feet.

Another question I have to wonder about is if this law covers the right to wear your lucky socks and underwear until your string of good luck runs out? Every good hunter and fisherman knows that there is a lot of luck involved in our sports, so we have to be able to take advantage of our good luck charms while we can. Just remember that most seasons are not really that long and if you air things out once in a while they don't get too bad. Besides if everybody does it no one will notice, of the rest of the hunting crew that is.

One of the other things we will have to check on with our legal staff is if a fisherman has the right to store worms in the top part of the refrigerator next to the leftovers and milk jug? Does it give us the right to store old animal parts and hides in the freezer with the wifee's frozen food?

They're sure are a lot of things in this law where you have to read between the lines to really understand all the protection us guys now have.

Please, let this be a warning to all you ladies out there. We men now have the power of the law on our side! It took a while, but it's easy to see what the real intent of the legislators was. If they keep passing laws like this to protect us males, including us lowly hunting and fishing males, I just may have to someday change my opinion of what goes on down there below the bridge!

Best of the Best Times

If I have learned anything from all the people I have met traveling around with my books it is the fact that the great outdoors is one of the best tools to use with your young hunting partners. It will bring more enjoyment to both of you than anything else will.

Did you ever stop and think of how good a youth can be shooting a target and yet how excited he can be when that first bird takes off right in front of him? There is just no way you can get someone ready for a feeling like this.

But I don't care if you are nine or ninety, there is something about the excitement that goes through you when you are waiting for a flock of ducks to come in or you just saw that flash of brown off through the trees and know a deer is working it's way toward where you are sitting. If the excitement ever goes out of hunting, I will hang up my guns and find something else to do. So seeing you only get to hunt a few months out of the year I figured that the best job in the world had to be the one where you are out in the woods hunting all the time. For poachers that is!

Now when you stop and think about this can you understand a job where what you are doing has the same kind of excitement built into it? I always said that as a youth you played cowboys and Indians or cops and robbers then when you became an adult you just went and found a job where you got paid to do the same thing.

Here you got to sneak around in the dark, run without headlights, trying to catch someone trying to rob Mother Nature of some of her bounty.

You had fast cars, high speed boats, snowmobiles, airplanes, 4-wheelers, and all the other toys you could only dream of. You throw into this mix a bunch of young guys that never see the danger that could come out of some of the things they are involved with. You just have one of the most interesting jobs a person could have.

When you add into this mix the officers from the sheriff department, the state police, and the officers from all the local law enforcement agencies, what a crew you had out there all conspiring together.

I loved every minute of it and all the great people I got to work with.

Chapter 2
History of DNR Air Force

In looking over some old books with stories about the old Conservation Department I read up on the use of airplanes in the duties of a Conservation Officer. The article was written in 1947 and it really makes one think of how little some things have changed.

It started out by saying that the use of an airplane in conservation work was nothing new. In fact airplanes had been in use since the early 1930's. One of the first uses was on fire patrol to assist the men in the old fire towers.

At the start of World War II the Conservation Department lost its whole air force (one plane) when Army Air Corp requisitioned it for the duration of the war. This was not really any problem because during this period almost all the air fields around the state were closed anyway.

Right after the war the department purchased two airplanes suitable for use in conservation work. A plane suited for this type work must be rugged, a good performer, and economical to operate. It has to be a high wing type plane with good visibility. It was often necessary to operate out of small, unimproved fields, and emergency strips throughout the state. For this reason it had to have the ability for rapid climbing in order to get over any obstructions at the end of these runways. Yet for reliable aerial observation, the plane should have a slow cruising speed, and likewise a low stalling speed, and a resistance to spin. These planes always had to be able to change their landing gear to skis or floats.

After World War II a lot of new equipment was available from surplus government equipment like an aerial camera, improved two way radio equipment, and field glasses.

As I stated up above, at this time the Conservation Department had already been using the airplane for fifteen years, but now they had a lot of new equipment to use. They no longer had to draw a crude map of the area, or make a crude note with the information about a forest fire or illegal activity on it and drop it in a weighted bag to the officers on the ground. Now they had two ways, short wave radios. Could we in this day and age of computers even picture a pilot writing a note, placing it in a weighted bag with a long streamer attached, and then trying to drop it close enough to the officers on the ground to get the fire report to them? Now all the planes, cars, fire equipment, and field offices were connected by radio.

With the use of the airplane the officers were now able to find and check large beaver dams to see if there was any activity around them. They could also check both rivers and streams and later in the year ice fishermen with the aid of the airplane. Areas that used to take all day to just walk in and check were checked in just a matter of minutes now. The officers in the field were finding a whole new way to get orientated and acquainted with the area he had been working for years. Lakes, streams, logging roads, deeryards, beaver ponds, could all be checked out and spotted from the air now.

They now used the airplane for illegal deer hunting patrols, the opening of pheasant season, and checking commercial fishermen. The plane was used to check lakes during the closed season and to check some of the trout streams during the early spring fish runs. The list of the uses of the airplane goes on and on.

Back during this period the conservation officer ranks were filled with young men who had served in the war as pilots, therefore there was no shortage of qualified pilots for the department to use. From this group of young men the pilots for the conservation department air force were chosen.

The goal at the end of the articles states, "The day should not be far distant when each protection district in the state will be assigned a plane."

But, something must have happened to cause a change of heart because it seems that the DNR air force has went in the other direction in the last few years.

Chapter 3
The DNR Air Force

I guess you would have to say that I received my first taste of the DNR Air Force even before I worked for the Conservation Department. While still attending Michigan Tech I had to go to the Marquette field office for the then Department of Conservation to interview for a fire officer job. While sitting in the upstairs conference room with a group of men asking me questions, a party came running into the room yelling, "Our controlled burn is no longer a controlled burn!" All the men interviewing me jumped up to run out of the room leaving me sitting there all by myself wondering what was going on.

A short time later they all came back into the room and the interview started up again. It no sooner got a good start than the same man came running back into the room once again yelling, "Our airplane at the control burn just hit a power line!" Once again all the men interviewing me ran out of the room leaving me by myself.

A few minutes later they once again returned to inform me that the plane had hit a power line taking part of the tail section off, but it was all right and able to land safely. I finished the interview and took a fire officers job down in Caro on the Thumb.

After getting to Caro I received my second taste of the DNR Air Force. Right after arriving at Caro the Regional Fire Supervisor in Lansing sent a twin-engine airplane assigned to the Lansing office over to fly us around our area of responsibility. As we cleared the runway I realized the airplane door next to me was not latched. Needless to say I informed the pilot of this fact and he told me, "Don't worry the door won't come open with the wind blowing so hard against it." Great! It's just what I wanted to do, fly around the area for an hour in an airplane without the door latched! But we made it and I never fell out.

Later on I was to learn that the pilot that flew us around that day had trouble with his landing gear while trying to make a landing with this same airplane. After this accident there was an investigation and it was found that this full time DNR pilot for one of the DNR planes out of Lansing did not even have a real flying license! But I did hear he had a learners permit from years ago. All the years I knew this pilot, who from all accounts he was a good one; nobody had ever managed to check to see if he was a licensed pilot by asking to look at his pilot license.

What Road?

When I transferred to the U.P. I was to come to know a couple more of the DNR pilots. I think both of these were from the old school and took their pilot training along with Snoopy. Needless to say if you have read my other books I had the good fortune of being able to talk my way out of ever flying with either one of these two pilots.

They were both super pilots for the job they had and it was unreal some of the things that took place. To this day I cannot believe some of the things they could see from the air in the dark along with some of the things that happened.

I can remember one time when I was sitting up in the Thunder Lake Road area near where what we called the A-frame Road was. The pilot got me on the radio and told me to head down the A-frame Road he had spotted a shiner down there working a sand ridge. I drove down the road and after about three miles of running without lights he told me to flick my lights on for a second. I was then told to head back the way I had come because I had missed the road the shiner was operating on. I head back and after going about half way back I was informed once again I had missed the trail the shiner was on. I went back and forth two-three times and told the pilot there was not a road there off to the West. He told me, "Yes there is I can see it." I was then told to drive down the road slow with my parking lights on and he would tell me when I came to the road. I drove real slowly and all at once he said, "Right there! Off to your left!" We turned on a spotlight and sure enough you could see where someone had taken a big, four-wheeler over some small jackpine onto an old skid road to get onto a sand ridge to go shining. Sure enough as we waited out came this big-wheeled pickup that had been shining. How in the world our pilot could see a road in the dark of night from the air that we could not even find on the ground was beyond me, but he did.

The main problem I had with the other pilot was that he could see shiners and roads all right, but had trouble seeing rivers! I don't know how many times he would lead me into an area where some shiners were working only to find out that we were on the wrong side of a river to get to them. Do you realize how frustrating it is to get within reaching distance of the vehicle that is shining only to find out there is a river between you and them, and there is no way you can get to them?

....

Don't Look Now!

I guess there is nothing worse than being a supervisor and having to stand somewhere to watch one of the people working for you do something that helps your hair to turn gray a whole lot faster. On this day we were working over near the Blaney Park area looking for a lost hunter. This hunter had already been out in the woods for two days and one night. As is usual, we called in the DNR plane to help us look for this lost hunter.

When the plane arrived in the area the pilot made a number of circles over the area without any luck in locating the lost hunter. The pilot then called on the radio to ask if we knew anyone that could ride with him that knew the area between River Road and M-77? I told him that the man that owned a good chunk of the land that we were searching was down here with me at the patrol car. After a little bit the pilot came back over the radio to tell me he thought he could land in the field on the corner of River Road and North Gulliver Road. I took one look at the size of this field and where it stood and had one thought! You got to be kidding me!!

I called on the radio and ask the pilot, "Are you sure?" He told me it would be no problem. So he came in over the trees and set it down in the field. This was not really a problem for this pilot; for one thing you can be sure of, what goes up must come down. The pilot picked up his passenger, turned the plane around, and taxied to the far end of the field near the edge of the woods. I stood on the blacktop and listen to him wind up the engine of the plane until I thought the engine would take off without the rest of the plane. Then here he came, off across the field toward where I sat on River Road. Everything looked great; he was picking up speed, going in a straight line and should take off all right. It was not a matter of getting a second chance! You either make it or it is bad news, but everything looked great up to now.

He got to the point where he should be leaving the ground when everything went wrong! Just as he should have left the ground he hit a dead furrow near the end of the field. This made the plane take an instant right turn to head sideways right for the power lines off the end of the field, between the field and the road! I about had the big one.

I will have to say that it is the first time in my life that I ever saw a plane take off sideways from a runway, only to have it's wheels clear some power lines by the amount of wear there was off the tires. But he made it, and I told him to drop the party off at the local airport when they were done and I would gladly give him a ride home. For some reason after what had happened the pilot thought it was a good idea.

A Good Night To Stay Home

One thing you have to remember is that a lot of our flying in the DNR patrol planes were not done under the best of weather conditions. When you understand that most poachers like to use the weather to their advantage it is no wonder that the pilots are ask to fly when just maybe they should stay at home. But you do have to remember that it is always up to the pilot whether they decide to fly or not.

In the fall of the year one of the main things you have to worry about is fog. In fact we were always told to warn the plane if ground fog came into the area where we were sitting. On this night we were sitting waiting for the plane to get up, when it finally did. We had told the pilot the fog was bad, but he thought he could make it up all right and still look for shiners for us to check out. Right after he got airborne it seemed he called us on the radio and told us he was going back in. I later heard the rest of the story.

It seems our pilot was asked to fly a night patrol for us over Schoolcraft and part of Mackinaw County, so he ask the District Supervisor to ride with him. The weather was on the bad side with a light rain, but the fog was not to bad. Yet. As I said, we waited and the plane finally got airborne. But as darkness came the fog got really bad. The pilot had the lieutenant with him on this night patrol and after they flew for just a short while the lieutenant realized they could not see a thing, especially the ground and the things on it! When he realized this, he said he hit the pilot on the shoulder and told him, "Put this sucker down! Head back for the airport!"

The pilot turned the plane around and headed back for the Newberry airport. After flying for a while and dropping lower and lower, the pilot turned around and yelled back to the lieutenant, "Can you see anything of the airport?" Do you know the feeling that goes through ones body when the pilot asked his passenger about finding an airport in the fog because he has no idea where it is?

On this same night in the same area another airplane hit a radio tower and crashed while trying to find the same airport. But once again our guys came through all right.

Some of the Best Guys There Were

I will have to admit that of all the old game wardens I ever worked with, the pilots for the law division were some of the best officers there were to work with.

One time we talked our local prosecutor into going up with Air-4 one night to see what it was like to fly night patrol looking for poachers. They spent a couple of hours up there and I guess the prosecutor had a whole different outlook about looking for poachers from an airplane. It is truly amazing what you can see from the air.

You have to remember that for years the number one activity, around Schoolcraft County here in the U.P., was getting a scanner to listen to the

DNR plane trying to catch shiners on the weekends. You would be amazed how many people you would meet on the street during the week that could tell you who you checked with the aid of Air-4. They could even tell you where the most active areas were.

I often wondered if it was such a well listened to activity, how come so many people still went out and tried to get away with it? Could it be that, "I never will be the one to get caught!"

Do you realize how many times poachers were caught out trying to get an illegal deer the first night they owned their new rifle? Some things in life just do not make much sense.

Chapter 4
The Art of Getting Stuck

I guess if you plan to do your best and try your hardest at everything you do; it would only make sense that when you get stuck, and you find you are really stuck. This is the way it was with me. It was not to often that I got stuck, but when I did it was a bummer.

I Came By It Naturally!

When you grew up over in Ontonagon like I did, which is famous for it's Ontonagon red clay, it is only a matter of time. As a kid while hunting with my dad he had an old bug made out of a Model-A. This bug had larger tires on it, no body, but a wooden box built on the back. We would take this out hunting on all the old railroad grades and back roads. If you have never seen a mud hole up in this country you have really never even been close to being stuck. So most of the time if the beaver had a road flooded you just stopped and looked for a way around it. Sometimes there was nothing you could do but pick the best spot and just go for it. This was the case up on Deer Creek Road one day.

After looking over the area of a beaver dam that had flooded the road, Dad would say, "Get back in and hang on, we are going to have to try and go right thru it." We got back into our bug, Dad would back up a couple of hundred yards, (remember it was just a 4-cylinder Model-A) and off we went. Our plan and our goal were to get enough speed so we could get from one side of the beaver pond to the other where it covered the road. All went great, until we got about two-thirds of the way across the water that now was our road. All of a sudden there was this piece of tree that the beaver had cut floating on the water! There was nothing we could do now; we were already committed to trying to make it across this water that covered the road.

Here we came skipping across the water doing great, until this piece of log disappeared under the front of our bug. Then all of a sudden the front end of the bug rose up off the road and we stopped rather suddenly. Out in the middle of the pond, where it was wet and muddy. What else could you do but get out of the bug into the water and try to figure out what had happened.

Here we found that this floating piece of log had gone up into the area of the A-frame of our old Model-A bug. When this happened the other end, both ends were pointed seeing a beaver cut them off, went down into the mud to lift the front end of our vehicle up off the ground. Back in those days nobody had a winch or a com-a-long like most people do now, so you went to plan B. There was nothing you could do now but make plans to sweat, get wetter, muddier, and hope you could get unstuck before dark came.

The only jack you had was a little screw type made by Mickey Mouse. I guess this is the reason my dad was one of the first people in the world to own one of those four foot jacks when they came out. But we didn't have one with us today. We had to block up the front of the bug and then dad had to lay down in the water to try to cut the log off that was holding our bug off the ground. Needless to say we finally got out, but one of the first projects after getting unstuck was to cut a road around this beaver pond so we didn't have to try once again to drive through it.

I can only remember one time we got so stuck we had to walk out of the woods. On this lucky day we had mom and all the kids with us. Dad took turns carrying all the kids out of the woods on his back, but it was the last time I can remember mom ever taking that golden opportunity to go hunting with us back in the mud hole country using our old hunting bug. But you had to do this because everybody knows that the best hunting is always where you can't get to under normal conditions.

Almost, But Not Quite!

One of the first things a person learns that drives these back roads, where the road is missing to be replaced by a large mud hole is, "You are never really stuck until you stop!" As Long as you keep moving, you may slow down to a crawl, but just keep moving and never, never completely stop!

One of the other things I was to learn real fast from one of the old timers I worked with was, "It is hard to get two tons stuck at 60 miles an hour!" You put these two lessons together and you have, "Floor it and don't stop no matter what!"

It works most of the time.

Did you ever wonder why most State Troopers and Sheriff Deputies wear wing tips or other dress shoes? Really the reason is that the management higher up is really trying to tell them never to get off the blacktop roads! Especially if I happen to be riding with them.

On this day I was riding with a deputy and we were checking along Lake Huron for some lost fishermen. We were hitting all the two-track roads that went down to the lakeshore so we could see if there was anything along the shoreline. We had covered a number of these roads when we came to one that followed a creek and then came out at the lake. Just before we reached the lake, with no place to turn around, we came to this large mud hole all the way across the road. It covered the whole area from the edge of the woods to a creek bed that ran parallel to the road.

In my mind I never gave too much thought to this mud hole. You see most mud holes if you were to rate them from one to ten, this one would not even be a good four.

We stopped for a second and then the deputy started through the water leading up to the real deep parts of the mud hole. When we dropped off the solid part of the road into the mud and were really committed my deputy friend panicked. We had already reached the point of no return, when he yelled, "We aren't going to make it!" and started to slow down. I yelled, don't stop now! Don't stop!" But the damage was done. We stopped all right, right in the middle of the mud hole. A nice white patrol car, two officers in uniform, with low quarter shoes. Here we sat with mud and water all around us. The lesson learned is, once you are committed you had better hope you make it to the other side!

....

A Tree too Far

As I have stated a number of times, in twenty-five years while working as a game warden I have got stuck very few times. But, when I did I usually did an excellent job of it.

On this day I was on patrol by myself in the national forest. The road I was traveling on was a good solid road, so this was not a problem. But after traveling a good ten miles I came across an immovable object. All the way across the road from the woods on one side, to the low swampland woods on the other side, was this large White Pine tree that had been blown over by the high winds. There was no way I could ever cut this tree out of the way with my little axe. But just maybe, I could cut off and move enough of the branches from the top of the tree to get around it. This plan put me on the swampland side of the road.

You see one thing I hate to do is patrol an area where you have to backtrack through the area you just patrolled through. So I went to work cutting some of the branches off this tree. I got an area opened up and looked everything over. The land off this side of the road was a low, wet spot with a lot of Tag Alders in it. But on this day I had a 4-wheel drive pickup so this should really be no problem. I started out in low range, working my way off the road into the ditch. I got the truck lined up parallel to the road between the treetop and the swamp off to my right. It worked perfect, except...

Just when I had this large White Pine tree right off my driver's side door, I suddenly realized that the ditch was a whole lot lower on the passenger side than on the driver's side! Just about this time both passenger side wheels sank into the mud, sliding sideways until I was now firmly resting against the trees in the swamp with my passenger side door. Bad news, even if I could move I did not dare for fear of the damage I would do to the truck. In fact one tree had came to rest right where the box of the pickup meets the cab. So, if I kept moving I would do serious damage to my truck, so I stopped. In a system of one to ten as far as getting stuck goes I just scored a perfect ten!

One thing you have to understand is, no red blooded, all American male is ever going to get on a radio to call for help after getting stuck. Life just does not work this way; it is kind of like a guy admitting he is lost. So I went to work.

First I tried to jack up the front, and then push the pickup off the jack up the hill to make some room between the pickup and the trees it was resting against. If I got it off the trees then I could see if I could drive out. The key word is uphill! It just usually does not work to jack something up and then push it off the jack going uphill. After an hour or more of work I was to prove once again that this theory of physics would not work. Now to plan B.

I figured if I could cut the trees that were against the passenger side of the truck I could work my way out. You see I wasn't really stuck, I just couldn't move. So I started to try to cut off these four trees. After another hours work without really making any headway, I figured I had better come up with plan C. So I did.

From the back of the truck I took out all the chain I had in it. I stretched this chain out on the road at the front of the truck. I laid it out going across the road to the nearest large tree, I then pulled it back to hook on the front of the pickup. All was going well, and this is a better theory than either A or B were so it really should work out. At this point I took my four-foot jack out and laid it at the end of the chain on the far edge of the road. You noticed I said the far side of the road. Most roads even here in the U.P. do not have trees growing on the traveled portion of a road!

O' great! Here I found out that sometimes things that look so promising when they start out can soon come to a sudden stop. After laying out all my chain, and the jack, I found that I was three feet short of being able to reach the tree. You have to remember that I had to try and pull the pickup almost sideways to get it off the trees. At the same time going up out of the ditch without hurting the truck in any way.

So I went digging through the back of my truck. Nothing! I then looked under the seat in the cab. Nothing! I then took a chance and walked down the road to an old campsite on the bank of the Fishdam River to look around. The only thing I found here was an old cotton clothesline stretched between two trees. I cut it down and headed back for the truck seeing it was all I had.

Returning to the truck I took my clothes line rope and went around the tree, back to the jack, around the bar on the jack, and then back to the tree. I did this five-six times until I ran out of rope. It was now or never for plan C. I was either going to be able to pull a pickup, sideways, out of a muddy ditch, or I was going to have to admit failure. Then my only choice would be to get on the radio to call for help. The jack clicked, the chain and rope raised up off the ground and everything tightened up. About this time I said a little prayer and kept working the jack. Little, by little the truck started to move sideways. I had to repeat this part of the project three-four times before I got far enough out to take a chance on driving the truck back up on the road. But it worked! Once again I did not have to get on the radio to let the whole world know I had messed up and got stuck.

....

Almost

Well, in the spring of the year there is one big problem that you have to watch out for. After the snow goes and things start to warm up the frost comes out of the ground. When this happens you can really get stuck. Twice I had problems with this.

In both cases we were going to check something out when all of a sudden we realized that we were sinking through the sod on top of the ground. Slamming your vehicle into 4-wheel drive you just tried to keep on going. All the time hoping you would not sink far enough into the ground so you bottomed out. When this happens you usually have no choice but to make a big circle around the opening. As your subconscious minds keeps saying, "Please keep moving, please keep moving until we get back on solid ground, please."

If someone was to see this take place all they would see is mud flying as you kept the pedal to the metal trying to keep going. I can remember after one of these trips around a field going into a car wash and the owner was not to happy with all the mud that had built up under the vehicle. But, he did let me wash it.

There was the time when this happened, and to add to the problem, I ended up in the ruts left from a logging skidder that had crossed the area. Man, was I in trouble! I floored the old International 4x4, "Corn Binder," I was driving and just kept on going. The engine was screaming and any minute I expected to see pistons come up through the hood as we made our way slowly forward. We did make it out of the ruts onto solid ground, but the only problem was we were on the other side of the mud hole from the county road. We still needed to get back through this bad mud hole to get out on the county road once again.

Going back we took our time and scouted a way that kept us on high ground and out of the skidder tracks.

I guess getting stuck goes with the job. But one soon learns a lot of little tricks of the trade to help him along in his travels on these old 2-track roads here in the U.P. When these tricks don't work, his other sack of tricks better be able to get him out once he messes up.

....

Only a Trooper!

One day I was working on a poacher that had built an underground pit on the side of a sand hill off a power line to hunt from at night. We had a 4-wheel drive pickup back in this area looking for evidence. You came into the area on a pretty good 2-track, but then you had to turn up a power line to get to the top of the sand hill where the pit blind was. The 2-track up the power line was all sand and really even less than a 2-track.

But you guessed it! Here came this trooper to help us out up the sand hill along the power line in his bright blue car. We just looked and thought, "There is just no way he is ever going to make it!" And he didn't. Pretty soon sand started flying and the trooper's patrol car settled down onto the frame in the loose sand. There is a time when you are stuck, then there is a time when you are really stuck. He was really stuck. There was no way we wanted to call for a wrecker so we got our great minds together.

I always carried a long rubber rope like the ones used to tie up ships in my truck. We got this out and hooked one end up under the patrol car. We had to shovel a place so we could get under it first. We then took this long rubber rope and ran it around a big pine tree off to the side of the power line. We continued along until we got the other end on some solid ground. Here I backed up my pickup truck and hooked the rope to the back of it. We were ready!

Now remember I wanted to pull him back onto the 2-track road to solid ground, but I could not pull him straight without getting stuck myself. So here I was pulling to the west while hoping the trooper's patrol car would head south. The rope tightened and stretched around the tree and back to the trooper's car. As the trooper spun his tires slowly we pulled the car out of the holes and backwards down the hill. We had to re-hook and change our angle two-three times before we got the trooper's car back on a solid road.

It is amazing what you can do with a piece of rubber rope and some geometry that you wondered why you ever had to take.

Chapter 5
Dad, Tell The Truth Now

I had a party tell me a rather interesting story a while back when I was at an outdoor show down state. It makes one wonder about life and you have to decide who was right or wrong. As the father was talking, I soon realized that we both knew this old game warden. I had worked with this older officer, who had served as a game warden for fifty years in the same area. The dad went on to tell me this story.

It seems that dad had taken his young son on a hunting trip with him. The son was old enough to go out with him, but not old enough at the time to purchase a bear license. (This was before we got caught up in this mess we have now with the bear permit drawing system.) The two of them headed up to the western part of the U.P. to spend some time together and do a little hunting.

They spent time setting up after finding a place they thought looked good. All during the week there were bear moving around the area where they were hunting, but they never had any luck in spotting a bear. It seems that nothing would come in when they were sitting there waiting on it. Finally the week of hunting was over and it was time to pack up to head back home. They were not the least bit sorry, because they had a great time together even if they had not seen a single bear.

As they were heading out on their way back home, all of a sudden a bear ran across the road right in front of them. The boy saw it first and yelled to his Dad. They got out and the dad got his gun out so they could walk down the road to see where the bear had crossed. As they came to the spot in the woods, there off to the left side of the road stood the bear. Now, if you are a bear hunter, you know that this in itself is unusual. Most bear once they are scared and start to run don't stop until they are long gone.

The boy asked, "Dad, can I shoot it?" The Dad figured why not, the boy had shot his rifle enough times before. So he handed his rifle to his son who then shot the bear.

It turned out to be a real large bear. In fact it was so large that after they returned home the story about this big bear being taken was soon going around town. During the course of this time the story came out in the paper, with a picture of the big bear. It also told the fact the son had really shot the bear. What a story, a father and son go on a hunting trip and his young son shoots a record bear. Everybody likes to hear about it, well not everyone...

It seems as the story got around some "zell-its in Lansing who all of a sudden realized, according to this article the boy was the one who had actually shot the bear. This and the fact he was not old enough to be legally hunting bear.

As the father told me, "It was not too long after the newspaper story was published before this old game warden came by the house." He said you could tell right away he did not want to be there, but had been sent over to check out the story everybody had heard by now. The father told the game warden what had taken place. He said that his son had shot the bear after asking him if he could, as they both stood watching it.

The old game warden told the father, "I tell you what, if you just tell me you shot the bear I can go on my way and that will be the end of it." The father told me you could tell that the warden felt like he was between a rock and a hard spot. The officer did not want to end the memories of this hunting trip this way, with a ticket. So he repeated, "Just tell me you shot it."

The father replied, "Sir, I know what you are trying to do and I am grateful, but I can't do it." He went on, "You see if I tell you I shot the bear when I didn't, it makes me tell a lie about my boy and myself. I have always told him to tell the truth, that it doesn't pay to lie your way out of things. So I just can't do it."

So you see that both the dad and the game warden were caught between a rock and a hard spot.

So the Dad said, "Go ahead and write me a ticket and I will take care of it. We will just add it to the story of the great time I had on this hunting trip with my boy."

Chapter 6
Little Quirks

As you travel through life working as a Game Warden you come across some interesting things. Right or wrong they make life seem strange at the time and sometimes you just have to laugh at them. Here are a few of the strange type of facts that a Game Warden may encounter in this day and age.

Bug Spray

It was a warm morning in the early part of summer when Eino and Teivo were walking around the yard. They came to the corner of the yard where Eino had a few apple trees planted. As they looked over the trees they found where there were a few bugs on the leaves that should be sprayed. Eino told Teivo, "No problem, I'll just run down to the hardware to get some bug spray."

Only after having arrived at the hardware does Eino realize how many different kinds of bug sprays there are in the world. Lucky for Eino on the back of the jar is pictures of different type bugs each spray will work on. He finds what he needs and heads home.

Later while sitting on the back porch he decides to read the label on the jar to see how to apply his bug spray. This is really not a problem, because there are only three-four lines telling you how the bug spray works. But then as Eino keeps reading he comes across an interesting fact. There may only be three-four lines telling you how the bug spray is to be applied and should be used. But, wait a minute can you believe this, there are two pages of directions telling you what to do with the empty jar once you are done using it!

Eino was just wondering if the user is less important than someone who may come across the empty bottle later on? If this bug spray container is so bad should not the warning be part of the directions for application too?

Florida Refrigerators

While still working as a game warden I was on a trip down to Florida with my family. If you have ever been along the ocean or the gulf you will see a lot of fishing piers going out into the water. In the area where we were they had built a new four-lane bridge across the gulf to connect it with some of the islands. When they did this they left the old bridge standing for fishermen to use. Both ends of this bridge were blocked off so you had to walk out on it if you wanted to fish from it. The bridge itself was over a couple of miles long and there were always people out on it fishing.

On this trip across the bridge we observed dozens of fishermen trying there luck. One of the girls with us, from the cold land up north, now in the hot land in Florida, thought that the state of Florida really was helpful to those that were fishing. As we rode across the parallel bridge she looked over at the fishermen, saw a number of these little buildings along the old bridge for the fishermen. Seeing these there she said, "It sure is nice that the state of Florida put those refrigerators over there for the fishermen seeing it is so hot down here."

There was dead silence in the car as everybody looked at one another and thought, should we tell her what those little buildings really are or just pretend we didn't hear her? But I guess the looks and the silence got to her and she soon realized that those refrigerators were really Porto-potties.

I have to tell you another tale that was given to me after someone read my book A Deer Gets Revenge." This guy's better idea almost got him in real trouble.

It Almost Got Me!

This party that I am telling about in this story lives over near Trenary, so this may have something to do with what happened. It seems that all of us hunters have to come up with a plan just in case we ever get the really big one.

Myself, I usually take one of the kids little plastic sleds to pull the deer out on. That is if I should be lucky enough to get one. I cannot remember my Dad ever dragging a deer out. During this time period the hunting crew would hang them in a tree out in the woods where they were shot. Then when it came time to break camp they would take the old horse used for skidding logs out from the farm and pick the deer up as they brought their camping gear out of the woods.

The guy in this story had a plan in the back of his mind also. In fact it went a little farther than his mind, he was all prepared to use it just in case. As luck would have it, he did get a real nice buck, with a large rack the first part of the season. He dressed the deer out and set forth to use his perfect plan.

He had taken into the woods with him some rope to pull the deer out with, but he had also taken a large piece of plastic. First he placed the front legs of the deer up on the deer's antlers and tied them there. He then laid his trophy deer on this piece of plastic and then wrapped it around the deer a number if times. He then used a short piece of duck tape to hold the plastic in place around his buck. A nice neat job and it really looked like it should work! He took hold of his dragging rope now tied around the deer's antlers and started dragging his buck out to the road. His plan worked just like he figured it would. The deer slid along on the new snow as smooth as could be and he hardly worked up a sweat as he worked his way toward his car.

About half way to his car he had a little ravine, maybe not a little raven, but surely not a big one, to cross en route out. He pulled his deer, wrapped in plastic, over the brink of the ravine and headed down into it. This project was working real slick and there was hardly a need to pull on the rope at all. In fact he was not pulling on the rope! In fact the rope was loose in his hand! In fact, as he looked over his shoulder, he saw that his trophy buck was about to attack him with his antlers coming right at his back!

Our deer dragger, now a deer runner, took off running down the hill of the ravine with his buck in hot pursuit!! As he saw this was not going to work, he finally jumped off to the side of the trail he was on landing flat on his face. Just as he cleared the trail his trophy buck went flying by taking part of the leg of his hunting pants with it. Caught to his buck's antlers was part of the material from his pants leg, as it continued to the bottom of the hill. He never did tell me who got out to his pickup first. I can just see it now, "Hunter attack and hurt by dead deer!"

....

U.P. Missing Smelt Association

When I first returned to the U.P. to work you would not believe the smelt there were and what a zoo it was during the smelting season. There was regular villages set up at some of the better smelting creeks or rivers across the U.P. Some people would spend a week to ten days just camping at these streams to visit with friends and maybe even catch a few smelt. When they did run you could fill up a five-gallon bucket with one dip. But for the last couple of years all you get to do is sit around the fire to talk about the good old days and how it used to be. After the way smelt fishing has been the last few years Eino and Teivo came up with a better idea....

Eino and Teivo's better idea is explained in the letter below.

Howdy all you disappointed smelt fisherpersons out there,

Well I guess we are just going to have to form an organization called the U.P. Smelt Association. Or would a better title be the U.P. Missing Smelt Association. Eino has more people call to ask him if the smelt are running yet, each spring. Usually he has no idea. The way it has been the last few years you may hear where someone got a few, but it surely is not like it used to be in the good old days.

Eino figures if he and Teivo formed the U.P. Missing Smelt Association, they could charge $20.00 a year membership. With these dues they could then purchase some hats and bumper stickers to let everybody know about their group. This along with the concern they had for all those homeless, missing smelt. Then they could hire one of those Exspurts to write a report and apply for a Federal Grant to study their problem of the missing smelt. Then naturally they would form a committee, because every official above board organization has to have a committee or two of Exspurts working on the problem whether it even exists or not. They understood that it is important to do this even if you never come up with an answer to the problem at hand.

Now let's see, 100,000 members at $20.00 a membership, which comes to a whole lot. Then the cost of hats and bumper stickers comes to, taken out of that whole lot. This leaves a lot of the whole lot of money left for the party. The organization will send out a bi-yearly news letter to all the members in the two stamped, self addressed envelopes, they are to supply with their dues each year. This yearly newsletter will inform all members where our annual meeting is to be held and what to bring.

This annual meeting of the U.P. Missing Smelt Association would be held each year on the bank of one of the creeks where the smelt used to run. Here they would have a big bond fire on the creek bank. Then ever once in a while one of the members will run down to the creek to make a couple of dips to try to see if just maybe the smelt have returned. It is important to keep in practice just in case. Plus you would give the local game warden someone to check for a fishing license.

O' I forgot to tell you that there is a $10.00 penalty, on top of the regular $25.00 (You notice the $5.00 difference.) membership, for all Trolls that would like to join the U.P. Missing Smelt Association. This is for an associate membership that allows you to supply the Brats for the annual meetings. This because chances are we will have to forgo our plans to have a smelt fry seeing the smelt never seem to run anymore.

I sure hope you will take the opportunity to join our group right away. Remember there is a limit to the number of hats and bumper stickers we have because we have yet to order any.

The Good Old Days

If there is one subject you can talk about the "Good Old Days" on, it is the way smelt fishing has disappeared here in Yooper Land. It went from the small towns set up along the streams like I talked about in the story above, to this past year when you were lucky to see one or two cars parked along the streams looking for smelt.

There are those that tell me that there are still tons of smelt out in the big lake, but they just do not bother to run up the creeks like they used to. I have been told that with the low water for so many years the smelt out there now have learned to spawn along the shoreline in the shallow water. Could this be true? I do not really know, but they sure do not run up the creeks and rivers like they used to in years gone by.

The only thing I do know is that there is nothing like setting up a little two-burner gas stove on the bank of a smelt stream. Then catch a few fresh smelt, clean them right there and deep-fry them. Then I used to make up a hot sauce that you could dip them in and good eating had arrived. We would go through a lot of smelt out there having a ball in the evenings. Now it looks like something else that has went by the wayside. But who can tell maybe someday the "Good Old Days" will be back along the smelt streams along Lake Michigan.

Chapter 7
Only In America

Some questions and answers that were really ask in court during some trials. Of course if you work law enforcement soon certain lawyers, become some of your favorite people. You never really shed too many tears when you hear one of them mess up in court.

Q: What is your date of birth?
A: July 15th
Q: What year?
A: Every Year.

Q: What was the first thing your husband said to you when he woke up in the morning?
A: He said, "Where am I, Cathy?"
Q; And why did that upset you?
A: My name is Susan!

Q: And where was the location of the accident?
A: Approximately milepost 499.
Q: And where is milepost 499?
A: Probably between milepost 498 and 500.

Q: Officer, when you stopped the defendant, were your red and blue overhead lights flashing?
A: Yes
Q: What did the defendant say?
A: What disco is this that I am at?

Some winning questions:

Q: The youngest son, the twenty-one year old, how old is he?

Q: Were you present when your picture was taken?

Q: Was it you or your brother that was killed in the accident?

Q: Did he kill you?

Q: How far apart were the vehicles at the time of the collision?

Q: You were there until the time you left, is that true?

Q: How many times have you committed suicide?

Q: She had three children right?
A: Yes.
Q: How many were boys?
A: None.
Q: Were they all girls then?

Q: You say the stairs went down to the basement?
A: Yes.
Q: And these stairs, did they go up also?

Q: How was your first marriage terminated?
A: By death.
Q: And by whose death was it terminated?

Q: Can you describe the individual?
A: He was about medium height and had a beard.
Q: Was this a male, or female?

Q: Is your appearance here this morning pursuant to a deposition notice I sent to your attorney?
A: No, this is how I dress when I go to work.

Q: Doctor, how many autopsies have you performed on dead people?
A: All my autopsies are performed on dead people!

Q: All your responses must be oral, OK? What school did you go to?
A: Oral.

Q: Do you recall the time that you examined the body?
A: The autopsy started around 8:30pm.

Q: And Mr. Dennington was dead at the time?

A: No, he was sitting on the table wondering why I was doing an autopsy on him.

Q: Doctor, before you performed the autopsy, did you check for a pulse?

A: No

Q: Did you check for blood pressure?

A: No

Q: Did you check for breathing?

A: No

Q: So, then it is possible that the patient was still alive when you began the autopsy!

A: No

Q: How can you so sure doctor?

A: Because his brain was sitting on my desk in a jar!

Q: But could the patient have still been alive nevertheless?

A: It is possible that he could have been alive and practicing law somewhere.

In another section of my books there are a couple of stories about some of the things we ran into with lawyers while cases were being tried. It really makes it interesting and it leads one to believe that 99% of Americans have no idea how our court system really works. It is not really like on TV.

....

Only A Supervisor

The other day in my travels I came across Teivo and he was all worked up. It seems he was due for his yearly civil service evaluation. Somehow when he was taking out the trash he came across the report his supervisor had prepared on him and his job performance. So Teivo took the list over to Eino's house to see what he thought about it. He wanted to get Eino's input on whether he should be satisfied with the report his supervisor was writing up on him. (P.S. All the statements made below were really on someone's evaluation report.)

The statements on the report went like this:

Since my last report, this employee has reached rock bottom and has started to dig.

His men would follow him anywhere, but only out of morbid curiosity.

This employee is really not so much a has been, but more of a definite won't be.

Works well when under constant supervision and cornered like a rat in a trap.

When he opens his mouth, it seems that it is only to change feet.

He would be out of his depth in a parking lot mud puddle.

This young man has delusions of adequacy.

He sets low personal standards and then consistently fails to achieve them.

This employee is depriving a village somewhere of an idiot.

This employee should go far, and the sooner he starts, the better off we are.

Got a full 6-pack, but lacks the plastic thing to hold it all together.

A gross ignoramus--144 times worse than an ordinary ignoramus.

He doesn't have ulcers, he's a carrier.

I would like to go hunting with him sometime.

He would argue with a signpost.

He has a knack for making strangers immediately.

He brings a lot of joy whenever he leaves the room.

When his I.Q. reaches 50 we should sell.

If you see two people talking and one looks bored, he's the other one.

A photographic memory, but the lens cover is glued on.

A prime candidate for natural deselection.

Donated his brain to science before he was done using it.

Gates are down, the light is flashing, but the train isn't coming.

He has two brains, one is lost and the other is out searching for it.

If he were any more incompetent, we would have to water him twice a week.

If you gave a penny for his thoughts, you'd get some change back.

If you stand too close to him, you will hear the ocean.

One neuron shot of a synapse.

Some people drink from the fountain of knowledge, he only gargled.

Takes him two hours to watch 60 Minutes.

After reading this over Eino had to admit it was better than last years evaluation. Plus a whole lot better than the one he received before he got promoted to area supervisor.

A doe with antlers

Could that be blood right between its eyes?

Chapter 8
Best Friends

By Cathy Walker

I clearly remember the day as if it was yesterday. I had just arrived home from a friend's house, when as I walked through the door of my house I found a beautiful, copper-colored puppy prancing around our living room floor. His tail was wagging so vivaciously that it was causing his whole back-end to swing with the momentum. At our first meeting his big, glossy, brown eyes reflected the joy, which was obviously evident in my own eyes. From that very moment Rocky and I were best buddies. It was thought that we were inseparable.

Although my family was not looking for a dog when we got Rocky, things fell perfectly into place, allowing him to live with us at that time. Some friends of our family had wanted Rocky to be their son's dog, because his dog was getting older and did not have much time left to live. Things ended up not working out as planned, since their son was not ready to replace his beloved dog, so Rocky came to make his permanent home at our house much to my delight.

As a child, having a dog with as much energy as myself could not have made life better. From the time I would come home from school, until my mother would say I had to come into the house and clean up, Rocky and I would play outside. We would play endless games of fetch, hide-and-seek, and tag. It was though our energy would never run out. It was the same everyday; Rocky would be outside waiting for me to come home from school. It was as if he somehow knew what time school got out, and when I would be returning home. He would run up to the car jumping up and down, looking at me through the car window. His eyes seemed to be pleading with me, begging me to hurry up and play with him. It was the same every day for the rest of my elementary, junior-high, and high school years. After staying outside with Rocky for hours, my mother would call me in to get ready for dinner. Then as I would take my place at the dinner table Rocky would take his place in the doorway of the living room, just outside of the kitchen. Rocky had quickly learned that my mother's law of "No pets in the kitchen" meant he had to stay out. Though Rocky had quickly learned this rule, he had also quickly learned how to get as close as possible without crossing the boundaries. In fact, Rocky was quick to learn both my mother's house rules and a unique way all his own of getting around them. Although my mother often got irritated about having to constantly clean up the dog hair, feed Rocky when I forgot, and let him outside on cold winter mornings; Rocky soon melted her heart with his brown eyes, the same as he had with the rest of my family.

Then came the day when I had to leave for my first year of college. Saying good-bye to Rocky was not as bad as I expected it to be. Everything was so exciting that I did not have time to think about missing all of our good times together. However, Rocky did not forget, after I was gone, he would still run up and down the stairs to my bedroom wondering where I had gone. During the nights my parents could hear him running around the house looking for me, trying to find where I was hiding.

Then came the winter that Rocky's arthritis developed. He did not run like he once had, he would walk, and his walk was even slower than it once was. It eventually reached the point where it broke my heart to watch him struggle to his feet after he had lain down. That was how Rocky was when I came home the first summer after my freshman year of college. Although Rocky tried to be as active as he had been back in our younger years, he just did not have enough energy. It did not take me long to realize that I was probably saying good-bye to Rocky for the last time when I left home to return to college after my summer vacation.

I was right, that was the last time I was to see Rocky. And now when I think of Rocky, my eyes well up with tears as I remember my faithful dog. Though I have to smile when I think of all our wonderful times together. And I must agree with the person who said, "That a dog truly is a man's best friend."

Chapter 9
Modern Math at Work in the Woods

Teaching math in 1950: (PS. I was there!)
A logger sells a truckload of lumber for $100. His cost of production is 4/5 of the price. What was the logger's profit?

Teaching Math in 1960:
A logger sells a truckload of lumber for $100. His cost of production is 4/5 of the price, or $80. What is his profit?

Teaching Math in 1970:
A logger exchanges a set of "L" of lumber for a set "M" of money. The cardinality of set "M" is 100. Each element is worth one dollar. Make 100 dots representing the elements of the set "M". The set "C", the cost of production contains 20 fewer points than set "M". Represent the set "C" as a subset of set "M" and answer the following question: What is the cardinality of the set "P" profits?

Teaching Math in 1980:
A Logger sells a truckload of lumber for $100. His cost of production is $80 and his profit is $20. Your assignment: Underline the number 20.

Teaching Math in 1990:
By cutting down Michigan's beautiful forest trees, the logger makes $20. What do you think of this way of making a living? Topic for class participation after answering the question. How did the forest birds and squirrels feel as the logger cut down their trees? There is no wrong answer.

Teaching Math in 1996:
By laying off 402 of its loggers, a company improves its stock price from $80 to $100. How much capital gain per share does the CEO make by exercising his stock options at $80. Assume capital gains are no longer taxed, because this encourages investment.

Teaching Math in 1997:
A company out sources all it loggers. This saves on benefits and when

demand for their product is down the logger work force can easily be cut-back. The average logger employed at the company earned $50,000, had 3 weeks vacation, and received a nice retirement plan and medical insurance. The contractor logger charges $50 an hour. Was outsourcing a good move?

Teaching Math in 1998:
A logging company exports its wood-finishing jobs to its Indonesian subsidiary and lays off the corresponding half of its US workers (the highest-paid half). It clear-cuts 95% of the forest, leaving the rest for the spotted owl, and lays off all the remaining U.S. workers. It tells the workers that the spotted owl is responsible for the absence of fellable trees and lobbies Congress for exemption from the Endangered Species Act. Congress instead exempts the company from all federal regulations. What is the return on the investment of the lobbying cost?

This was sent to me via E-mail and I have no idea where it came from, but just maybe there are others out there that like me wonder about how things are going in our world today.

....

Computerized Moose

If you have enjoyed my books and the way I write it is sure no secret how I feel about the Exspurts of this world. If you are a normal, red blooded, Yooper there just must be some inborn instinct about this. Here are some facts that will help bare this out.

With all I have to do in life I can honestly say that I have never played one of these "Keep score" computer games. Who in the world cares about this little guy running around, jumping high buildings, walking on water, and all those other things he does, just to sit in front of a computer to play games? Life is to short and time to valuable to waste it doing this.

But there is one computer game that I did find rather interesting. I guess they must have used this modern math. Let me see now, two negatives make a positive, right. So if two of something are missing, the negative, that must mean that there are four of these something's out there some-where, right?

Well it went something like this.

Some people sure are Lucky! Did you hear the news that the Exspurts in charge of the Moose program in the U.P. lost most of their moose? It seems that there are hundreds of moose unaccounted for up here in the U.P. The counters sure are lucky they didn't have a Mom like I had! I can just hear her now, "Now, John where did you have them last?"

It seems like when they flew their annual moose count one winter they came up with about one-third of the moose they should have found. They even went back and tried to recheck things and still could not come up with the amount of moose they felt should be out there.

Now, I may have lost my mittens or the likes, but how can you lose a 1,200-pound moose? And worse yet a couple of hundred big moose? It will be interesting to see what really happened, if this was just one of those things that happen and the count was just off or if something really did happen to the moose. From what I understand, most of these moose that are missing did not have a tracking collar on them, so they cannot use this method to try to locate them.

If all this is true, and what I hear also is true, it may have been a stranger winter than we thought. From what I now understand the tale goes some-thing like this. You bring in some moose to the U.P. Before you know it the moose are doing what moose are suppose to do so you get out your lap top computer.

Now, if two moose do what moose are supposed to do, you should have four moose someday. Then if this increase of two is plus two females, which now makes three, and once again the moose do what moose are suppose to do before long you have ten moose where once you had only two.

But, maybe of these ten you now have three males, but you also now have seven females. So once again spring arrives in Yooper Land and would you believe it, on your lap top computer you now have twenty-four moose running around out in the woods. It is hard to believe the way this moose herd is growing.

But, like so many of us the day finally arrives that we find out that these moose like so many of us are computer illiterate! On your lap top computer you have generated all these moose, but out in the woods where things really count they just were not there.

I was never the best at math to start with, I sure am glad I never had to use this modern, computer-generated math that is out there.

....

Modern Geramedy

Now, in order to figure some things out in life you have to figure the curve of the ark, multiply it by the force behind the object, and then time all this just right. This is a true tale that could only happen to a Yooper.

Would you believe this if it were your fishing pole you had lent to someone? It seems there was a crew of young people going out fishing. One of the youth did not have any fishing gear so he borrowed a fishing pole from his buddy's dad. (Now just maybe an X-buddy's dad) They were down in one of the fishing holes where the highway runs over the river right near their fishing hole.

It seems that our still learning fisherman was trying to cast under the bridge to see what was lurking in the deep, water under the shadows of the bridge. Our fisherman could not quite get his line to go out to where he wanted his lure to land so he could work it through the area where just maybe the big one was waiting. Try as he might things were not working out.

He finally backed up a little bit farther, swung back with both hands on his buddy's, dad's borrowed, fishing pole and let her rip. Away it went!! The lure, the line, in fact the whole pole!! It cleared the water, cleared the side railing of the bridge, and landed in the middle of the highway just in time to be run over by a passing car!!

I can hear it now, "But! Dad it wasn't our fault! You see if that car hadn't been using the highway just when the pole landed on the road we would have been all right."

....

One Plus One Could Be Too Many

I have to sometimes laugh at the way things have gone in life since the time game wardens were issued patrol cars until this modern age.

You see when we were first issued patrol cars we could only have the one radio antenna mounted on our patrol car. There was just no way we could even have a radio in the cars because you would have to have another antenna on the vehicle. As one supervisor said, "What do you want to do, look like a porcupine out there?" I had to admit that personally I had never seen a two-quilled porcupine in all my travels. But, this did not matter only one antenna per patrol car.

Besides what would the public think if they thought a state employee had a radio in his patrol car! After all if the radio was there he might listen to it when on duty! This was life in the Stone Age.

But have times ever changed in the new computer generation. Now they have antennas coming out of every corner and even the middle of the roof!

First you still have the same old radio antenna. But now you can have a radio with an antenna, plus the antenna for the car phone you now have, plus another antenna for the lap top computer you use to check on the guy out there who quit school in the fourth grade to take up violating.

Now all this would not be so bad if the game wardens still drove a full size car for a patrol vehicle, but they don't anymore. All this equipment with its half dozen antennas is all mounted on a pickup truck!

I just don't understand where this world of modern math is going?

If all else fails

Chapter I0
Tree Stands For Game Wardens

I guess working the area where I worked for so many years with the flat, marsh lands, I find it rather interesting when the "Big House" fought so many years to keep firearm hunters from hunting from scaffolds. One thing I have always found interesting is the fact that just one person for or against something, sitting in the right place, can stop something from happening for years. This was the case of making scaffolds legal for firearm hunters. Michigan was about the last state to make this legal.

One thing they were to find out after making it legal to hunt from trees with a firearm, was the fact that not everybody ran up a tree. In fact I think with the cold weather in the U.P. and the fact that if a party already had a good, successful hunting spot they were not about to change it.

Hunting from a tree, should we make it legal? The one key word in this statement is the word legal. In this flat, marsh country, here in Schoolcraft County, hunting from a tree would be nothing new. So if the big worry for the DNR is hunting accidents caused by allowing rifle hunters to legally hunt from a tree, I suggest they do a study here in Schoolcraft County.

The real question and debate here would be, "Does the fact that you are now legally hunting from a tree make your chances of falling out of that tree higher than if you were illegally hunting from a tree?"

The following points dispute the arguments that the DNR has as far as the dangers of hunting from a tree go.

(1) If there were going to be a rash of accidents because of people falling out of trees, would not Schoolcraft County already have statistics showing this? I have not heard of any accidents where a rifle hunter was ever hurt during a firearm-hunting season while hunting from a tree. Of course this could be because the thick layer of pine needles or the marsh grass under the tree works like a mattress when you land on it. So therefore maybe you should only be allowed to hunt from pine trees in marshland.

(2) If it were made legal would it not be safer to descend from a tree in a

normal slow manner, rather than having to jump from a tree in one flying leap. Or trying to leap and swing down from your illegal tree stand with sweaty hands while all the time you are trying to keep an eye on the game warden making his way through the woods toward you?

(3) If tree stands were legal, would not a person be more willing to remove a legal tree stand from the woods rather than having to explain how they were just a good Samaritan going around removing illegal tree stands? Because if legal they would use a good stand that may have cost them a few dollars rather than nailing a couple of pieces of wood up in a tree where they are out nothing if they have to leave it. I remember one season during the five day quiet time I saw a vehicle heading back into the National Forest with a large, old, wooden extension ladder tied to the roof. Being the normal game warden with a warped mind for some reason I assumed this party was just maybe going to be up in a tree when season opened. I was telling one of the other officers about this car with a ladder on the roof heading back into prime deer hunting country. This other officer looked at me and never cracked a smile as he said, "Well, just maybe he is going to use this ladder to get across a creek." You know I never thought of that with my inquisitive game warden mind. But if you believe this I have this nice forty, in a wetland swamp, with no legal access, in prime deer hunting country, I would like to sell you.

Well, I guess I will close with a tale about how effective tree stands are. When I was working in a flatland area where there was a lot of waterfowl hunting, I made good use of hunting from a tree. There was this one marsh that was rather large and had a lot of ways to get into. This made it hard to work even when we knew there was a lot of illegal activity in this area. So one year before a waterfowl season started I went in to look the area over and figure out just how I would work this marsh for illegal waterfowl hunters.

On one end of the marsh was a big beaver dam and right behind the dam was this monster White Pine tree. After checking things out I found that the best way to work the area during waterfowl season was to get way up in this White Pine, hide in the branches, and use a walkie-talkie. There I could sit up in this big pine tree to tell the other officers working the area just what was going on. It proved rather effective for two reasons: Deer are not the only things that do not look up into trees out in the woods, neither do duck hunters. Thank goodness ducks normally do not land in trees.

....

Be Careful of Those Trees

This week I am going to do something a little different in the old Fish Report. Someone gave me the following article that is so strange it is interesting. It is out of Ed Erickson's "The Drumming Log" which is a weekly outdoor article in the Iron River area.

It was titled: An Incredible Story

If all the pieces of the following story are true, it is one of the most incredible sagas of North America woods.

Pete Korach of Mineral Hill brought in a clipping last week that was printed in the "Deerwood (Minn.) Courier." The article was originally printed in a March 1976 issue of the Pine City (Minn.) Pioneer, a town just into Minnesota from Wisconsin.

"An investigation is underway at the University of Wisconsin to determine the historical value of a find recently made in the woods near Ladysmith..."

The story said two men; a Chapin and Walter Latsch were sent to Ladysmith by a Chippewa Falls firm, which had purchased stumpage on a tract of land nearby in the town of Murry.

These men "batched" in a rough shanty while cutting logs and cordwood for their employer. "Among the trees selected, they notched a large basswood and felled it. Though it had a large hole some 30 feet above the ground, they considered it good for several-foot logs," the article said.

"They struck their saw into the basswood at a point where they expected a cut would give them a 20-foot log. All went well until they were almost through the big tree when their saw evidently struck a rock. A cautious second attempt proved the futility of trying to saw through the log..."

By turning the log several times, the cut was completed and the log rolled away, "revealing what threw the two men in a bad fright, for there, staring up at them, was the ashen face of a man... they summoned enough courage to drag the body of the man from the hollow trunk and their worst fears verified, hastily set out for town."

"At first the men's story was laughed at...but a party of four men was secured and made the trip. And witnessed the ancient tragedy."

"There, encased in the living trunk of a tree, was the entire body of a man, fully clothed in homespun s and buckskins that fell away when touched. The head had been covered with long hair, which was tucked under a coonskin cap. With the mummed body in the hollow tree was an old muzzle loading flintlock rifle and a muzzle-loading pistol of fanciful design."

"In the pockets of the man's clothing, which was like ashes, was found several decayed bits of paper and a few French coins, which were dated 1164. The only clue of the man's identity was a scrap of officially looking paper bearing the name 'Pierre D'Artagnon' signed "Jacques Marquette'."

"....it is thought on good authority that in Rusk County had been found the body of Captain D'Artagnon, who was lost from Marquette and Joliet's party on a trip down the Mississippi in 1667.

"The solution to the body being found in the old basswood tree is advanced in the theory that D'Artagnon , pursued by the Indians, crawled into the hollow tree to hide and being unable to crawl out, died there.

"The peculiar action of the sap of the live basswood petrified the body and preserved it for the men to discover.

"The body was brought to Ladysmith where it was shipped to the state university," the newspaper clipping concluded.

Wha-a-a-a!!

Oswald's Bear Ranch

Are Lake Trout fillets suppose to have spear marks?

Let's see now, how many could I catch & keep?

Chapter 11
Don't Believe Everything You Hear

I want to take this time to let you in on a few things that have come to my attention in my travels through the state with my books. You would think that if you got caught with an illegal deer and it was going to cost you $1,000.00 plus the fine and cost, that people would find something else to spend their money on. This does not appear to be true. This past week I heard about over ten deer that had been killed illegally.

First of all let me once again put an "old wives tale" to sleep. People always tell you when you are a Game Warden that they would not care if the party hunting the deer illegally really needed the meat. If this were the case I would never report the illegal hunting. In twenty-five years of working as a Game Warden I could count on less than the fingers of one hand the number of times this proved to be true. It almost never is, and that's a fact. Talk to the law enforcement officers or the court to see how many times this is true in this day and age.

A while back there were two men caught with two illegal, little fawns they had shot in their car trunk. It seems that they shot these two small deer right at dark and came back three-four hours later to load them in their car. The Conservation Officer then caught them. In the car was enough booze, that if spent on food they would not have had to shoot these two fawns. Now they are looking at a $1,000.00 for each deer, plus fine and cost and maybe a few days in jail. They could also lose the firearm used and the car they were in. In fact in looking back over some old records, back in the 1930s and 40s they often lost their car when used in this type of violation.

While talking to an officer this past weekend I found out there has been almost ten deer found with just their hind quarters cut off and the rest of them left to spoil. Now someone that needs the meat bad enough is not going to do this. If ten deer were found this way how many have really been shot by these outlaws? Also this weekend I received another call from a party that came across a place where they feel a number of illegal deer have been butchered up. How many deer have been killed already this year right around our area?

Now real sportsmen are not shooting these deer!! But the thing is that a local Conservation Officer really needs help in stopping this type of activity. There are usually only two conservation officers assigned to work most counties in Michigan. A lot of their job keeps them from working all the time on illegal hunting. So, they do really need our help. If you call yourself a sportsman, you should feel as sick as I do when you hear about all this illegal waste of deer that is going on. For a few years after the big fines came out things slowed down, but now I feel that they have found out that they may never have to pay them off, so they are back out there. Lets help clean this up.

If you see or hear of any illegal hunting going on call one of the local Conservation Officers, or call the RAP number at 1-800-292-7800. Also remember that there is a very lucrative reward system for those that may supply the local game warden with some information of illegal activity that leads to some arrest.

Let me say a couple of things about something that may or may not take

In-line Muzzle Loaders

place. First of all let me say that my hat goes off to the state of Colorado for having the guts to pass the law that all states should. They outlawed the "in-line" muzzleloaders for the special muzzle loading deer hunting season. Now, being the old fossil that I am, I can remember when muzzleloading season was started. It was set up and meant to be for those that wanted to hunt with their old fashion muzzleloaders. You know a muzzleloader! Muzzle loader! This means that you were meant to load them from the muzzle like Davy Crockett did! It was part of the game plan, along with the miss-fires, wet primers, and everything else that goes along with real muzzle loading hunting. But once again we humans found a way to circumvent the law until what was meant to be no longer is because someone can make money off the change. Come on you Michigan legislators lets do what is right too and go back to a muzzle-loading season like it was meant to be!

Not Really, But It Sounds Good

It reminds me of an excuse I heard that was on an accident report one time. It appears this Conservation Officer was driving down a two-track road, not really watching what he was doing. The next thing he knew a medium size red pine tree had redesigned the left front fender of his patrol car. As he was making out the accident report he knew there was really no way he could justify what had happened, so he figured he would just give it his best shot.

"While out on patrol north of town, I was traveling down this two-track road going to check on a complaint. During the course of this patrol out in the woods, which with a conservative estimate, was made up of at least 219,456,783,894 trees, I managed to miss all of them but one."

"This single tree, of all the trees in this woods, that I was unable to miss, caused serious damage to the left front fender of my patrol car."

I never did hear if the excuse worked, but for some strange reason I don't think so.

There was another time, and this accident was a little closer to home. During this period someone in the Big House decided we should have light brown or beige colored patrol cars. They were bionically, ugly and looked like a two-ton, four wheeled mouse, running around in the woods.

One day while pulling into the driveway, the patrol car slid sideways on the ice and the top of the driver's side, back fender went under the mailbox. This mailbox was mounted on top of a piece of well casing pipe, which had a piece of heavy steel welded to it. This piece of steel had edges on it, so when it went over the fender onto the trunk of the patrol car, it left three-four groves in the fender. Man! What now!

When asked about the marks on the back of the patrol car, that were rather hard to miss, this story was relayed to the lieutenant.

"You are not going to believe this, but while out on patrol, with this super, ugly, mouse colored car, I was traveling down this two-track road. While going along in this mouse colored car all of a sudden an unusually large, Great Horned Owl, came swooping down out of the trees. Before there was really any time for me to take any evasive action this Great Horned Owl sank his hooks into the back fender of this mousy colored patrol car! The only thing I could do was to make a sharp turn, while flooring the patrol car to throw the owl off the fender. While doing this the talons from the owl caused the damage to the patrol car's fender."

The look on the lieutenant's face could have been one of those that would go down in history if it could have been captured on film. It kind of expressed the hopelessness for the officer standing there telling him this excuse about the accident.

The bottom line is, there can be a million excuses for our actions, but at the end we are really the one responsible for them.

Chapter 12
Guardian Angels

This is a true story that falls under the heading, "It could never happen to me". Where I used to work you spent a lot of time out on the big lake. We had a lot of waterfowl hunting, both sport and commercial fishing, and tons of pleasure boaters. During the fall of the year we would team up with the Federal Officers from the Fish and Wildlife Service to check waterfowl hunters hunting the flight ducks out in the bays of the great lakes. For some reason, back in those days, the federal officers had a lot better boats then we did to work the great lakes with.

The officer that I worked with all the time had been in the Fish and Wildlife Service for a number of years and had been a state Game Warden before that. He had spent a lot of time out in boats in some bad weather and waves you would not believe. One day I went to meet him to go to work and he asked me, "Did you hear what happened to me the other day?" I had not so he told me this story.

This officer and a couple of buddies had made plans to go out duck hunting. Now down there, the way you duck hunt is with a boat and decoys. You set the decoys out, pull a canvas cover over the boat to hid it, then wait for the ducks to come in. They had spent a little time and done a little hunting without any luck. So they planned to move to a different location out on the bay. They loaded up their decoys and turned the boat to move across the bay. As they turned with the wind now hitting their back, all of a sudden a big wave came over the back of the boat to fill it full of water. The boat went under water right now! Then only the hunters along with their decoys were left floating on the surface. They could not find any life vest and were in their heavy hunting clothes. So thinking quickly, they forced a number of duck decoys up under their hunting coats to help keep them floating. When they tried to swim to shore they found that the winds were now blowing off shore so strong they could not make any headway trying to reach the beach. They had been out floating in the water for a real long time now and it is a long way to the shore on the other side of the lake in the direction the wind was blowing.

In a cabin on the beach was a party watching TV. He later told the officer that for some reason he felt he should get up to use his field glasses to look out into the lake. He had a good set that he used to watch the waterfowl.

As he sweep the lake looking at the now real rough weather and waves, all of a sudden he observed some people out bobbing around in the waves! He could not believe his eyes! After he doubled checked he called for help and the hunters were rescued.

This is the only time I can remember this friend telling me anything about this experience. But you better believe that he had a better respect for the powers of nature and now did believe it could happen to him.

P.S. The boat was later recovered on the beach on the other side of the lake.

....

Watch Your Step!

If you have ever travels around the part of the U.P. that we worked you would sure see some beautiful country. Our area ran from the shores of Lake Michigan up to the shores of Lake Superior. Included in this area along Lake Superior was Pictured Rocks National Park. In this area were two-three rivers that ran into Lake Superior that trout ran up to spawn in the spring of the year.

When you take this backwoods area where nobody lives and top it off with some good trout runs you are bound to find people back there trying to take a few trout. When this happened, you of course have the game wardens out trying to catch them. In most cases the two-track roads that go back into the areas of these rivers are something else. There are mud holes big enough in some of these two-track roads to lose a full size vehicle in.

The way some of these areas were worked was for the officers to take a 4x4 back as far as they felt they could without being heard. Then they would find a place to hide their patrol vehicle and walk back into the mouth of this river in the dark. When I say in the dark I mean just that. You see you could not very well walk through the woods using a light while trying to sneak up on someone illegally taking fish. So you made your way through the woods along these rivers in the dark.

On this night there were two officers trying to get back into the area of the Mesquite River to check it out. In some areas along the path you tried to walk in the dark it is a long way down to the river itself. On this night it was darker then dark out there. Believe it or not there are nights that are dark, but you can see things pretty well once your eyes get used to the darkness. But then there are those nights when it is really dark, dark. This was one of those nights.

As these two officers were making their way along high banks of the rivers in the Picture Rocks area the officer in the lead all of a sudden felt that something was just not right, so he froze right where he was.

Could it be he had heard something down in the river? Did he get just a glimpse of a light through the trees? Just what was it that told him to freeze right where he was?

After waiting a good amount of time and not seeing or hearing anything else he got to wondering? Finally when he was sure there was nobody else in the area he switched on his flashlight on the trail right in front of him.

What did this officer see less then another step right in front of him? Nothing! Here he stood looking over the edge of what appeared to be a hundred-foot drop off into nothing in the dark! Less then a step more and he would have went airborne down to the rock below.

You talk about a cold sweat going over your body from your head to your feet you sure feel it about then. As you sit down right in the middle of the path you thought you were following you get to thinking? What in the world really made me stop all of a sudden without taking that one more step that would have been your last? What causes something to go through an officer's body out there in the middle of no-where telling him to do something that ends up saving his life?

If you know me you already know what I think. As I said in the title of this chapter, **"Thank Goodness for Guardian Angels"** especially those that are assigned to work with game wardens.

Chapter 13
Fact Of Life -Old Age

I guess one has to face it at times and remember that old age creeps up on all of us even the old game warden. I thought I would tell you a few signs of true old age for an outdoors person.

Fossils Verse Computerized Game Wardens

I used to get ask all the time why I retired so young from such a great job? As I told people, "When they came out with all this computer stuff to try to catch a poacher that quit school in fourth grade it was time for me to get out." As you read the items below you will soon see how a Fossil like myself looks at things and how a modern game warden of the computer age looks at the same thing. When you get done reading this you will see why it was time for me to get out, so I left.

Today	Fossil
1-Log On:	A fisherman checks the fire and adds a log to it
2-Log Off:	Fire is too hot, kick a log off!
3-Ram:	When you run into a tree out in the woods
4-Windows:	The things wifee wants you to wash during hunting season.
5-Download:	Throwing firewood off trailer into basement
6-Mega Hertz:	When you take the first deep breath at -40 degrees
7-Prompt:	Wifee reminding you once again about the windows
8-Floppy Disk:	A retired game warden's back
9-Hard Drive:	Right after the frost goes out of the ground
10-Byte:	What deer flies are really good at
11-Screen:	What you better have good ones of here in the U.P.
12-Infrared:	The remains of your bait pile after deer season
13-Chips:	Something with too many fat grams
14-Micro-chips:	Fat free chips
15-Mouse:	What you trap at deer camp
16-Modem:	What you used to do with cans with semi-auto 22
17-Keyboard:	Where wifee used to tell you to look for patrol car keys you couldn't find
18-Software:	Paper plates

19-Main Frame:	What holds the roof up at camp
20-Enter:	Come in
21-Delete:	What you would like to do with ideas from Big House
22-Pause:	What you do more and more of as the years go by
23-Home:	Where wifee and I live
24-Number Lock:	A combination lock

25-Random Access Memory: When you can't remember how much you paid for your new deer rifle when wifee asks.

....

Maybe Not That Bad After All

Well, I guess there will always be those out there that will not understand the way I write my tales. Sometimes there are mistakes that were not caught in my books that I sure wish were, but there is a style that I was encouraged to use when writing my tales.

If you think some of my mistakes are bad, here are some that were sent to me that others made on reports and in newspapers around the country.

1-Police begin campaign to run down jaywalkers
2-Drunk gets nine months in violin case
3-Include your children when baking cookies
4-Experts think school bus passengers should be belted
5-Typhoon rips through cemetery, hundreds dead
6-Red tape holds up bridge
7-New study of obesity looks for larger group
8-Astronauts take blame for gas in space ship
9-Killer sentenced to die for second time in 10 years
10-Stolen painting found by tree
11-Miner refuses to work after death
12-President wins on budget, but more lies ahead
13-Juvenile court to try shooting defendants
14-Cold wave linked to temperatures
15-If strike is not settled it may last a while
16-Kids make nutritious cookies
17-Local high school cuts dropouts in half
18-Man Minus ears waives hearing

19-Steals clock, faces time
20-Hospital is sued by 7 foot doctor

As you can see I am not the only person on God's good earth that has trouble with the English language. I thought you might get a kick out of these statements.

....

Why Do I Have Problems

Well, maybe this little piece will help to explain why I have such a battle sometimes trying to figure things out. Someone who likes to give me a hard time about my stories sent this article to me.

A language teacher was explaining to her class that French nouns, unlike their English counterparts, are grammatically designated as masculine or feminine. Things like "chalk" or "pencil" she described would have a gender association although in English these words were neutral.

Puzzled, one student raised his hand and asked, "What gender is a computer?"

The teacher wasn't certain which it was, and so divided the class into two groups and asked them to decide if a computer should be masculine or feminine. One group was composed of the women in the class, and the other, of the men. Both groups were asked to give four reasons for their recommendations.

The group of women concluded that computers should be referred to in the masculine gender because:

1-In order to get their attention, you have to turn them on.

2-They have a lot of data, but are still clueless.

3-They are supposed to help you solve your problems, but half the time they **are** the problem.

4-As soon as you commit to one, you realize that, if you had waited a little longer, you could have had a better model.

The men, on the other hand, decided that computers should be definitely referred to in the feminine gender because:

1-No one but their creator understands their internal logic.

2-The native language they use to communicate with other computers is incomprehensible to everyone else.

3-Even your smallest mistakes are stored in long-term memory for later retrieval.

4-As soon as you make a commitment to one, you find yourself spending half your paycheck on accessories for it.

So you see it is no wonder that this Yooper game warden from Ontonagon has his problems with the English language.

Chapter 14
Flyers Are Weird

Did you ever run into someone that you have to wonder about? I mean, besides when you look in the mirror to shave in the morning. This past week I did. There was this party where I was that had to be on his third lifetime, because there is no way you could pack all he has done into just one lifetime!

This party has been a state trooper, worked for the DNR, been a pilot for different organizations, and also has been and is a firearm dealer. Now he is an anesthesiologist. He is one of those guys that could sit and tell you "war stores" all night long. The only thing you have to figure out is in what lifetime did his stories take place. This man also worked with some of the same older Conservation Officers that I did. So it sure makes for interesting times when I get to spend some time with him.

I also ran into some of the now retired State Troopers that were working in Manistique when I first moved here. We had a great time talking about those "Good Old days." The only problem is, as you get talking and recalling things, you soon find out that a whole lot of those you worked with, as a bunch of young guys without a care in the world, have went to the Happy Hunting Grounds. It makes you stop and think for a minute.

....

Emergency Landing

Now this on a lighter note. It seems there were a couple of guys up here flying for the DNR. As they were going along and circling an area, they got curious about a certain area that they wanted to check out. On one of the old charts they had it seemed there was an emergency landing field from the second world war marked in the same area they were flying over. So they thought, their first mistake, that they would set their plane down on this old emergency landing field to scout the area out near it.

So here they came down through the trees to set down on this old landing field as neat as you please. As they were getting out of the plane one of them tripped over something on the ground buried under the years of old, tall grass that covered the field. As they looked, they found that the field was covered with stumps from where some jack pine had been cut off a few years before. Just maybe the map they looked at was a little older than they thought.

As they walked back down the field away from the plane to see what this old landing strip was like they about died or could have. It seems their wheel marks were right between the rows of stumps all the way down the field. They had only one, slight, problem! There was just no way they were ever going to be able to keep their plane's wheels between these stumps to take off from this same field. So here they sat with no place to go!

....

It Looked Good

On this cold, winter day we had been called out to go on a patrol with our snow machines on Bay De Noc down off the Garden Peninsula. We were going to check some commercial fishnets that had been set through the ice. There was no way to get out to these nets without being seen. During this time we had to worry about some of the natives getting up on the bluff overlooking the area we were going to work to shoot at the officers checking the nets. For this reason you had those officers that were going to pull nets if they were illegally set and those that were there to just back them up.

The officers in charge had called for Air-4 from our district to be over the area to back us up out on the ice. There were a bunch of illegal nets located and the officers from District 3 started pulling them. It usually took a while to pull gill nets up thru the ice and Air-4 decided to land on the ice near us while the nets were being pulled. On this day there was a state trooper riding along with the DNR pilot on this patrol. They first came low over the bay to check it out for a place to land and everything looked real good.

So here we stood out on the ice and watched Air-4 come slow over the edge of the Garden Peninsula to come toward us to set down on the ice. Lower, lower, lower, and almost on the ice and then they set down. As they hit the ice, they were soon to find out that the ice was not near as smooth as it looked like from the air. As we watched the plane touch down, it then rose back into the air only to touch down again. It did this about six times while also bouncing from side to side. But they finally made their landing and then taxied over to where we stood out on the ice in shock and rather glad we were not one of those riding in the plane.

The state trooper got out of the plane and he was about as white as the snow that covered the ice out on the bay. The pilot of Air-4 got out like it was just another day out on the range. If he was shook up, he sure never let anyone know he was. As I stood there the thing that went through my mind was the fact that they still had to turn around and get back off the ice into the air. I thought that I would be more than happy to be traveling home by snowmachine.

After the nets were pulled, they looked for a little smoother area to use for their takeoff and it went off without a hitch. The only thing I had to say was, "Better them than me!"

Watch For That White Scarf

I guess if you are my age you can remember the old television add for some airline where they talked about how good their airline pilots were. They told how long ago they got rid of those pilots that wore a white scarf around their neck to tighten up when they went into a dive. In other words they had professional pilots. Not those flying by the seat of their pants, barnstorming type pilots. I could relate to this add and there was no doubt these barnstorming type pilots still had a job, they were now flying for the DNR.

One afternoon there were a number of people flying with Air-4 over to Drummond Island. They were cruising along without anything to worry about, not a care in the world. All of a sudden the plane engine made a strange noise, sputtered a couple of times and quit with the prop fluttering to a stop.

There is one almighty strange feeling and dead silence inside the airplane. When you hear some strange noises only to watch the airplane's prop flutter a couple of times and then come to a stop!

Needless to say those in the plane watch their life pass before their eyes. That is all but the pilot wearing the white scarf. As the plane starts down, as unnerved as anyone could say it, as he reaches up to throw a switch, as he tries to re-fire the airplane engine, the pilot states, "O" I guess I forgot to switch gas tanks." Finally he gets the engine to crank over and finally starts up once again.

Needless to say those riding with him age at least ten years while all this was taking place.

....

Where Was It You Learned To Fly Again?

There was this officer that has been in a number of my tales just because he seems to get into trouble now and again with what he has to say.

On this morning he was to fly around his area with one of the DNR fire pilots. This party had been flying for a good many years and as the stories went he had once been a crop dusting pilot. I never doubted this because in my mind there is a lot of similarities between a DNR pilot and a crop duster.

As they were covering the area where the officer worked, he asked the pilot if they could fly over a couple of lakes where he knew there were some duck blinds. The officer wanted to see if there was any activity around these duck blinds before he took all the time to walk into the lakes to check them out. So he asked the pilot if he would take a few minutes to fly over the lakes so he could take a look at these blinds.

The pilot circled over the lakes and dropped down a little so the officer could take a look. Not seeing as good as he wanted too, and not being able to tell if there was any activity around the blinds the officer said to the pilot in a rather smart alec tone, "What's the matter, you scared to get down low enough for me to take a good look."

Before the whole phrase had even cleared his mouth, the plane went into a steep bank, falling out of the sky, to head down toward the water on the surface of the lake. Right over the lake surface, right toward the duck blinds, only to pull up right over the trees on the end of the lake at the last minute.

I asked this officer what he saw on this trip across the lake over the duck blinds? He said, "Five 12 gauge shells, three 20 gauge shells, a few old pop cans, sitting on the floors in the blinds." In fact he told me, "Man, if there had been any hunters in those blinds they would have come flying out both sides of it as the plane came screaming down at them."

He also said, "Boy, there is no way I am ever going to mouth off at this pilot like that again, he about ruined my whole day."

He also told me, "You have no idea how hard it is for the human body to function when your insides are up at about 3,000 feet and the rest of your body is flying about twenty feet off the water surface across a lake. Besides it is really hard to breathe when all your insides are stuck up in your throat."

You know when growing up I can remember being warned, "You know your mouth and what you say can get you into trouble."

....

And Maybe Passengers Too

I guess you cannot always look at what happens from a pilot's point of view. In this case you have to wonder about the passengers outlook on life.

On this day our DNR pilot was flying on a wildlife patrol with one of the biologist checking out birds nests. In the late spring they would fly on eagle and osprey patrol to check out their nests to see how many eggs were in them. Then if the eggs are hatched, they would check to see how many little birds were in each nest for their records. Now you have to understand how big these birds really are. Some of the adult birds are huge.

On this day they were flying around an osprey nest trying to see how successful this nest had been. There appeared to be a couple of young birds in the nest that were almost big enough to try their skill at flying. As the pilot and biologist were circling the nest they must have got too close for comfort.

All of a sudden one of the adult birds came streaking out of the sky to attack this other large bird that had gotten too close to it's nest. Here came this large, adult, osprey in a full dive to crash into the wing of the DNR plane and remove a section of it. Needless to say this was not good if you were riding in the DNR plane, but it was even worse for the bird that tangled with the airplane.

As the pilot of the plane fought for control with a section of the wing missing the only thing the biologist could think of was, "I think the osprey might be hurt!"

The pilot said he yelled back, "The bird! How about us and the plane?"

Chapter 15
Friends?

The old group of game wardens (Conservation Officers) was a group of guys that really had a great time together. Some of the things that took place were the type of prank that one family member would pull on another. This is if they thought they could get away with it. Some of the things that happened made for some interesting stories when we got together at refresher school. Maybe the stories got better the more they were told, but this is the way I remember some of them.

Project Elf

Let me start off by explaining what Project Elf was so you can understand the drift of the story. Years ago there were plans by the US Navy and the Defense Department to build a high-tech radio system to contact the Navy's nuclear submarines here in the U.P. of Michigan. There was a lot of talk about it, but nobody really knew just where in the U.P. this radio system was going to be built.

There was this officer in the District next to the one where I worked that just had a natural way of being involved in a lot of pranks, or anything else that happened to other officers. You could sit for hours and tell tales about some of the crazy things this officer was involved with. This officer transferred to a new area and had purchased some land with plans to build a new house. He had told the other officers in the area where he planned to build and in fact had taken some of his buddies to the property to show them just where the house would be built. He even showed them how the layout of the house would be. He had big plans.

A short time later he came out to his property. As he pulled in, he saw where a survey line had been cut across part of his property. He got out and started to walk this line and check the survey stakes that were driven into the ground. As he walked he soon found that the survey that had been laid out went right through his property. In fact right into the area where he had planned to build his new dream home. As he looked the area over where his home was to be built, he found that some stakes were laying out where a building was to be built. In fact where a Project Elf bunker was to be built was right where the family room of his new house would sit.

He started to nose around and found that the stakes that came across his property, to lay out a building, were marked with the Project Elf name on them. He was floored! It seemed that the Navy and Defense Department with their plans for Project Elf were planning on occupying the same parcel of land his dream home was to be built on! He was livid to say the least.

You would have to know this officer to understand just what his reaction would be.

This officer felt he had only one recourse; he got to a phone and called the air force base at K.I. Sawyer here in the U.P. to find out what was going on. He then got some phone numbers to call people in Washington at the Defense Department. He called not just his elected officials in Washington, but just about everybody else in Washington he could get a phone number for. He finally got some satisfaction. As he told me, "I may have been the only person in the U.P. that ever saw the top secret plans for Project Elf." It seems that he really stirred the pot with all his calls about the survey line through his property for Project Elf. In fact things got so worked up that the U.S. Navy sent an Admiral out to Michigan's U.P. to meet with this officer to assure him that there were no plans to build part of Project Elf on his property. This Admiral had the Project Elf plans with him to prove it.

Things finally settled down after the officer felt assured his nitch here in God's Country was safe for the building of his dream home. But was the truth of these survey stakes and the layout for Project Elf really settled? It seems little by little the truth came out.

It seems little by little this officer found out that it was not the Defense Department and the U.S. Navy that had cut the survey line and placed the stakes for Project Elf across his property. It seems that it was one of his fellow game wardens that had felt this would be a good way to get even with this officer for some of the things he had done to them. The only problem was he never dreamed that the whole Federal Government would get involved! Once the officer that owned the property got making his phone calls the other officer figured he had better make himself scarce. So even though he had cut the survey line, placed the stakes, and laid out the Project Elf bunker right where his buddy's family room would be in his new house, he dared not tell anyone now. Too many phone calls had been made and too many people were now involved.

When I heard this story, the officer who got "stuck" told me, "I have to admit they sure got me good on this one!"

....

A Real Trick

As I have told in a number of my stories years ago game wardens would spend a lot of nights traveling around the area they patrolled without ever using their headlights unless they stopped someone. The only thing was when working this way plans had to be made so each officer knew where the other officers were patrolling. It would not be good to have too many patrol cars running around the same area without using their headlights.

For example if there were more than one car out on patrol they would divide up the area. One car would be assigned to patrol north of US-2 and another south of US-2. Still another might be assigned west of M-77 and so on. This is the way it was done and it was a cardinal sin to leave your area and head down into another officer's area.

But we all know there are always those people that get bored with the area they are assigned too. In fact if nothing is going on in his area it just must be that all the action is in another area. On this night there were two cars out on night patrol. One car was assigned to patrol north of US-2 and the other to the south of US-2. It was a perfect night to patrol without head-lights, or just to find a good spot to sit to wait for shiners.

As the night went along, and it was a rather quiet night, the officer work-ing north of US-2 got rather bored. After sitting for a couple of hours he decided to move around and in doing so broke the Cardinal Rule of work-ing without headlights, He decided to travel south of US-2 into the other officer's area. After all it is a big world out there and what is your chance of finding the exact spot where the other officer is patrolling. So here comes the north officer down a road running without headlights in the south officer's area. He had been driving around for a little while when he found himself going down this road when all of a sudden a little voice in his mind seems to say, "Turn on your headlights!" In fact this feeling was rather insistent! So he reached down to switch on his patrol car's headlight! There right in front of him, sitting crossways in the road was the emblem of the other patrol car!

He told me, "All I saw was this bright emblem reflecting in my headlights, a set of eyeballs as large as fifty-five gallon drums and getting larger, and another game warden trying to stand up in the front seat of a patrol car, while pouring a cup of coffee from his thermos at the same time."

He then said, "The only thing I had time to do was turn left, going off the road into the ditch, through a fence, and around the other patrol car."

The officer in the other car told me, "I would have done him in if I could have got my hands on him!"

They laugh now, but they were not laughing for a couple of seconds on that night.

Do We?

One day we were sitting upstairs at the old district office having a cup of coffee and holding a short meeting after the opening of duck season. As we were talking about how things had went for the opening of waterfowl season those that had worked the area told us what they had run into. One of the officers that worked for me made this statement, "The only real violations that I ran into out there was unsigned duck stamps."

I guess this is one area of violations that have always interested me. First of all when I started working as a game warden nobody really cared about unsigned duck stamps. If you were to run into one while checking hunters, you would just give them a pen to sign their duck stamp with. Then it seemed that the Federal Officers from the Fish and Wildlife Service made up their minds that this was a real serious law violation. So they started to enforce it. If you ask them why all of a sudden they felt this was a big deal and tickets were being written instead of having them just sign their duck stamp in front of you they said, "We feel they may be passing duck stamps around to other hunters to use instead of everybody buying their own."

I had two problems with this type of reasoning. First of all having worked the big waterfowl hunting areas around Saginaw Bay where you could check hundreds and hundreds of waterfowl hunters, I never knew of the using of waterfowl stamps by others as being a big problem. How could this be a big problem if they are glued to the hunting license of the hunter you are checking? In other words if the stamp is glued to one license it cannot be passed around.

The other thing is, most officers that worked waterfowl hunters knew the reason some hunters did not want to sign their waterfowl stamps was the fact that they collected the stamps. If they collected waterfowl stamps, they did not want their signatures written on it. The feeling of the Fish and Wildlife Service was, "Let them buy more than one duck stamp if they want one to collect." I had a problem with this type of reasoning also.

So as we sat in the district office talking about waterfowl season violations and the fact that the "biggy" was the unsigned duck stamp, I said, "Ok, lets everybody in this room that waterfowl hunts and has a stamp get it out." You see I knew a good number of the game wardens sitting in the room at this time were waterfowl hunters. I was asked, "Why?" I said, "Lets just all get our waterfowl stamps out and look at them." Again I was asked, "Why?" And some of them were not about to pull their waterfowl-hunting stamp out of their wallet to let everybody look at it. In fact they told me, "To stick it in my ear!"

So I ask, "I bet most of you don't have yours signed either do you?" They admitted they did not and the reason was that after the season they put them in their collection.

So you see I have a real problem making a federal case out of something that most people working the field think is of little meaning, so don't do it on their own waterfowl stamp.

A blind used for illegal night hunting

Chapter 16
Family?

I guess you would have had to be around during the "good-old days" to understand what I mean when I say that the people that made up the old Conservation Department were like a family. In the fast pace of this day and age I feel we have lost a lot of the things that made life great back when I was just getting started in life out in the "back-then" fast lane.

When wifee and I, along with our six-month-old son, arrived at my first assignment, one of the first people I met was Harold the game biologist. Now here I am in my early twenties just starting out my adventures through life and here is Harold at the other end of the game of life. He was in his sixties, but had the laughter and wit of someone my age. I guess if everybody could travel through the path of life, and still keep the attitude that Harold had we would solve a lot of the problems we have today.

Here are some things that happened with Harold's help.

There was the time that Dave and I were still fire officers in charge of the field office maintenance. In the winter months it was our duty to check on the upkeep of the fire equipment then paint and repair anything that needed it on the inside of the building.

During this time of the year when you had two young guys trying to find something to keep them busy they often had to work on some creative ideas. We had one heated stall next to the office itself where we usually had coffee with the rest of those assigned to this field office each morning. Dave and I figured that for something to do we should clean up this area and paint it up so it looked more like a coffee room.

Now you have to remember that in those days you had only a few colors of paint to work with. There was red and black for the fire equipment. There was battleship gray left over from the navy. Then there was dark green from the parks and the others divisions that used this color for everything under the sun. Of course there was white for all the walls inside and out.

So we set out on our project. First we painted the floor battleship gray with a black strip to walk on between the doors on both sides of this garage. We then took and repainted the coffee counter cupboards the normal white with a gray trim. Now understand that the coffee counter was maybe only eighteen inches by twenty inches at the most. We looked at this little area where the coffeepot stood and thought we should dress this up a little. So we mixed up some of the fire equipment red paint with some of the white wall paint and guess what we got? The prettiest pink paint you ever saw!

So we painted the coffee counter pink in a field office. We were natural born interior decorators this room looked really neat when we got done. In fact it looked so neat that Harold and his secretary went out and bought a little pool table to set right in the middle of the garage floor. Now this was one of those pool tables that shot marbles. But not when the story got to Lansing about the nice rec room the Caro Field Office had.

In fact when the story about the pink counter got to Lansing it went from an 18" coffee counter to the whole floor being a pretty pink, with a pool table! Things had grown to a full size pool table on a pink garage floor in a state building! Needless to say when this happened something caused the fan to malfunction.

I always said that the news of Harold and his pool table took a couple of weeks to travel from our field office to Lansing, but only about thirty seconds to travel back in the other direction telling us, "Get rid of that pink paint right now!"

Family Life in a Field Office

One day I was at the field office catching up on some paper work. I was now working as a Conservation Officer. I had been there a little while when Harold came in. Harold's office was in the back of the building and I used a desk in the front. During the time I was there I noticed that Harold walked into the area where I sat two-three times and then went back to his office.

After about an hour Harold walked up to where I sat and said, "John, I hate to tell you this because I was going to wait until you found out for yourself, but maybe you had better look under the front seat of your patrol car."

Knowing Harold like I did after working around him for a number of years I went out to check under the seat of my patrol car. What did I find? Here I pulled out an old, frozen, car-killed cat!

As I went back into the field office Harold told me that he had found this cat laying in the road a couple of days before on the way to work. So he had picked it up and put it under the seat of my patrol car. But as the days went by he got to thinking about what might happen if I didn't find the dead cat for a while. So he figured he had better tell me so it could be removed.

It Always Pays To Be Safe

There was the time that Wifee and I, along with the boys, were over at Harold's house to visit with Harold and his wife. They were just great people to spend an evening with.

During this evening visit with Harold we were talking about some hunting adventures. In the course of our talk we went into his back office so he could show me his favorite shotgun. It is no secret that back then if you didn't like to hunt and fish there was just no way you could ever get hired with the old Conservation Department. So we went into where Harold kept his guns. My two boys were with us as Harold got his pump shotgun out of his gun case.

As he pulled it out, doing something he had probably done a thousand times before, Harold pointed the shotgun away from where we stood to rack it to make sure it was empty. Out of his shotgun flew a shell to bounce off the wall and land on the floor!

I thought Harold was going to have a heart attack when this shell ejected from his shotgun. He could not believe it. As I picked up the shotgun shell off the floor, he kept saying, "I can't believe it, how could that have happened?" But what a lesson this was for my two young boys.

In the thirty years I have been teaching hunter safety I have used this little experience out at Harold's that evening to teach youth to always check to make sure a firearm is empty. I tell them, "Even if you already know it is empty, then leave the action open as you let someone look at your favorite gun."

A Chance To Get Even

Seeing Harold's wife was also a transplanted hillbilly the same as my wife we had a lot in common. So there was this time when my family had made plans to travel down to the Ozarks to see my wife's family. Harold heard we were going down to these back hills, so he asks us to bring a bag of grits back for him.

Now being a true Yooper I kind of relate grits to beach sand! I always told wifee that when as a youth you would be running down the beach, only to trip and fall and end up with a mouth full of sand, it was the same as trying to eat grits years later. But Harold wanted some grits, so I picked him up a bag down in Vanzant, Missouri. Of course there is one little thing that I have always had fun doing during the years. When I picked up this bag of grits I found a bag where there was enough room to have a little fun. Before I got home to take the grits out to the office for Harold I took a little pencil and perfectly changed the $1.75 that was on the bag to $7.75. I then took these grits out to give to Harold at the office, and never said a word about them.

About a week later at coffee Harold brought up the subject about the grits. He asked me, "John, have you bought many grits?" I told him no, in fact these were the first I had ever bought. He asked me where I got them and I told him it was one of those tourist stores down in the Ozarks. I left it at that.

Another week had passed when Harold once again asked me about the grits and said, "John, I hate to tell you this, but you sure got ripped off for those grits." I told him, "Really." So he told me that a bag of grits usually cost no more then $1.50 to $2.00. I just played dumb and never let on.

A long time later on I did tell Harold what I really paid for his bag of grits.

....

Who Me?

Well, all good things must come to an end and so did this working relationship with Harold Tubbs. It came time for him to retire when he hit seventy so a party was planned for all his friends to gather. A building was rented and all Harold's friends got together for one grand time before he rode off into retirement.

As the time for the party rolled around people started to come into the place for the party. There were friends from all over the state there. Harold was one of those people everybody just enjoyed working with. There were hundreds of people gathered around and all of them were visiting and waiting for Harold to arrive. His wife had come out with a couple of friends from church, so only Harold was missing. Missing from his own party that is. So everybody was talking with people they have not been able to visit with for a while, but by then almost an hour had went by and still no Harold.

By now people were starting to talk and ask, "I wonder where Harold is?" As a few more minutes went by people were all beginning to wonder? But everybody knew everybody else, except for a few of Harold's personal friends. The only person nobody knew was an older man with gray, curly hair, a bright-checkered shirt, and plaid, bell-bottom pants. Of course this was the sixties so maybe he was a throwback.

After about forty-five minutes with everybody getting a little worried now that maybe something had happened, Harold's wife walked up to this over aged hippy to reach up and pull off his curly, gray wig and there was Harold with us all the time. He had played the act so good even his secretary did not know "this was really Harold all the time. Finally the meal got started.

After the meal there were the usual gifts and credits for Harold and we had a great time. It finally came time for Harold to say something. He got up and thanked everybody for all the wonderful years. Then he had a gift he wanted to give to his secretary. He took out a little gift, wrapped in a jewelry box and gave it to her. She opened it up and here in a box from a jewelry store was a necklace. It looked like a stone on a gold necklace. His secretary picked it up and said, "It's beautiful." It was a big gold stone mounted on a chain as a necklace. Then she said, "But this stone feels so light." All of us from the office about died.

You see Harold had gone to Canada a few years before hunting and brought back this "stone". Harold had spent hours making this necklace. You see this "stone" was really a moose dropping with about three dozens layers of gold paint applied to it. Harold had then picked up a gold chain and box from the local jewelry store to make up this gift for his secretary. To this day I do not know if and when she found out what her beautiful gift really was. But I do have to wonder what the politically Correct Police of today would have done with poor Harold if this had happened in today's world, maybe life in prison?

Those days were what some of us call "the good old days". What a time we had working together for the old Conservation Department before it became the modern DNR.

Chapter 17
Great Minds

Ballistic Fishermen

If you have read some of my stories you would soon understand that as a game warden you sure run into some interesting people. In fact you run into some people that you soon make it a point never to run into ever again. This tale is about one of those never again type people. For a few years back in the early seventies it seemed that whenever we were out checking fishermen this party would be there.

The first time I ran into him was up in Grindstone City checking salmon fishermen. I had walked around checking a number of fishermen for their fishing license and asking how they were doing, when I came up to this guy. I walked up and said, "Conservation Officer, how are you doing? Could I check a fishing license please?"

Man! This guy went about six feet into the air just screaming! Before he even touched ground again the yelling covered from one end to the other about how he felt about the fact that this game warden had even thought of asking him to see a fishing license. The more he yelled the worse it got.

He compared us to the Nazi Gestapo, this being a police state, and a person might just as soon live in Russia! This was some of the good things that came out of his mouth loud enough for everyone from Caseville to Harbor Beach to hear. To this day I cannot recall how long it took him before he finally settled down and showed me his fishing license. But it did seem that it took forever.

It was not long before an officer came to know this guy and made it a point to not even go in the same area where he was fishing. One of the reasons for this was the fact you did not even have to ask him anything before he came unglued, just seeing a game warden was enough to set him off.

This is where we had our own way of having some fun. It seemed to never fail that if we had a recruit officer working with us checking fishermen we would spot this guy. It got so you would say to the new officer, "Why don't you go check those fishermen over there and I will check these on this side?" Off this new officer would go with a big smile on his face to check on the fishermen.

We would then find a place to just sit to watch what would happen. Up would walk this new game warden and ask this party to check his fishing license. We all knew good and well what would happen, this guy would just let loose. Up one side of the officer and down the other he would go. Usually the new officer would just stand there in amazement wondering what in the world set this guy off, as we would hide back in the trees about dying from laughter. You have to understand this would go on for ten-fifteen minutes before things would finally settle down.

Finally this new officer would return with a dazed look on his face and try to explain to us about this guy he had just run into. Our responses would usually be "Naw, nobody could or would act like that." Believe me this guy was worse.

Then came along the night that we had a chance to set him off into orbit. Of course there was no way any normal red-blooded game warden was not going to take advantage of this golden opportunity.

We came to check the night fishermen around midnight at Grindstone City. As we were walking around in the dark, we came across this pickup with a cab-high camper set up out on the end of the road along the cove. As you drove out here there were big signs on both sides of the road that stated in big red letters, "No Camping". But here was this pickup camper set up right there where you could not legally camp and guess who it belongs too? You are right!

I got my little instamatic camera out and we walked up to the camper. Now understand this was at almost one o'clock in the morning when we walked up to the back of this camper. I beat on the back of this cab-high camper and yelled, "Conservation officers, we want to talk to you!"

Even before the back opened up on the camper the yelling started. Then the back of the camper flew open. The party jumped up (I say jumped up, only maybe I should say, tried to jump up). With only his BVD's on, yelling all the time, as we light up the whole area in the camper with out big flashlights. If you were tall enough already to touch the top of the camper from a kneeling position you soon find out you have a serious problem.

Yelling all the time, trying to get into his pants, while bent in half, only to have us take a few pictures with our camera so we could prove he really was camping in a no camping area. If he always went off the deep end before, like I said at the start on this night he went into orbit!

As luck would have it, after just trying to do our job in a fair and unbiased manner, this guy was at the District Headquarters Office at Imlay City the next morning when the doors opened. We kind of figured we might have some explaining to do when he got done telling what happened.

But for once the law of averages was on the game warden's side. It seemed that our normal District Supervisor was out of town on this morning when Mr. Personality showed up and the Sergeant assigned to Lapeer was filling in for him. Now I will not say who this was, but every officer that ever worked this district knew about Officer Dave.

This party came into the office just smoking and screaming at the top of his lungs, only to come face to face with the Sergeant. For once he had come face to face with someone that could go word for word and expression for expression with him! Those that were around the office that morning said it was amazing to see. For years this guy had gone off on his tangent as the game warden's just stood there and took it, but not on this morning.

I was told as he left the office he was muttering something like, "Aba, daba, daba, said the monkey to the chimp, aba...

Then believe it or not I cannot ever recall running into this party again while working fishermen along Lake Huron.

....

Bet You Can't

It was a beautiful fall day that one of my boys and I decided to go out to do a little duck hunting. We had traveled up into the national forest to hit a few potholes and small lakes. We had spotted a few ducks when we decided to go over to check Wolf Lake for waterfowl.

We came to Wolf Lake and parked our vehicle back in the woods on a two-track beyond the lake. While getting our gear together we decided to set out a few decoys, then just sit for a while to see if any ducks came in.

Now Wolf Lake is shaped like a figure eight. One part is about five times as big as the other part is. Then you come to a real narrow part that goes between the two parts of the lake. We usually sat right off this narrow part so we could watch the ducks if they flew from one part of the lake to the other.

We got to the brush we used as a blind and decided to sit for a while deciding if we should set out any decoys. As the two of us were hiding there a small flock of ducks came down to settle on the bigger part of the lake on the far side from us. This is what you could figure on ducks doing. The only thing you could do now was to wait where you were to see if the ducks were going to work their way over to your side of the lake.

We had been laying in this brush-blind watching these ducks for about forty-five minutes when all of a sudden it sounded like the world had come apart at the seams. Off the two-track road that runs near the lake came a herd of big-wheeled, 4x4, pickups racing each other! Off around the lake right at the waters edge they roared, sending mud and dirt flying all over each other. They also sent our flock of ducks flying off for quieter places!

The trucks played games racing around the big part of the lake passing each other and seeing who could drive into the water the farthest without getting stuck. They finally came to the narrow spot in the lake right across from us and stopped. The only thing I could figure out now was that they were putting up a challenge to each other, "Bet you can't!" "Bet I can!"

Finally the challenge was taken and they climbed back into their trucks and backed up to the edge of the woods and aimed their mudder trucks at the narrow part of the lake. Right at where we were hiding in the brush. One by one they revved up their trucks to get ready to make a run off across the lake. All of a sudden here they came, hitting the mud and water at the edge of the lake then off into the lake itself. Tires spinning, mud flying, engines screaming, the challenge was on. Off across the lake they came to dry land once again and right into the lap of the local game warden who stood up in the brush just as they stopped to congratulate each other.

Needless to say the National Forest Service frowned on 99% of everything they were doing.

Sometimes Things Work, Sometimes They Don't

On this fall evening there were a number of game wardens working the Manistique area for illegal activity. We had checked a number of the trout streams that the fish run up without having too much success when we received a call from the state police post about a complaint at Thompson. We went by the post to check and see what the complaint was all about.

We were informed that they had received a call that there were some gill nets set at Thompson right off the mouth of Thompson Creek. They also told us that you could reach one end of these nets just by wading out off the shore just to the left of the creek. We headed out to Thompson.

We talked it over and figured that there was not much use in getting the boat from the field office. If we did get the Whaler we would have to launch at the Manistique River to make the run to Thompson Creek. Then we would have to try to catch the boat the gill-netters were using out in the dark running around Lake Michigan. It just would not work.

When we got out to Thompson Creek we looked around the left of the mouth and soon located the end of a gill net running from near the shore out into the lake. Needless to say there was no way of telling whom the net belonged to from what we found. So we had to come up with a better idea.

Our plan was to pull the end of the gill net which was closest to shore up onto the shore. We could get the net about fifteen feet up on the beach. We then took our old International 4x4 and backed it up to the end of the net. The net was then hooked onto the back of the pickup and our plan was set.

This was our theory if we could hook the net onto the truck, then wait until the illegal gill-netters had pulled enough of the net into their boat. Remember they were pulling from the other end. We would then try to pull them and their boat up on shore. In order for our plan to work the net in the boat would have to tangle up on something in the boat in order to pull them up to shore. But this was the best plan we could come up with.

Finally while sitting in the dark we heard a boat come into the area of the gill net. We listened as we heard some talking and figured the gill net was being lifted. I walked out into the water of Lake Michigan with a big flashlight to wait. When we figured they had to have almost two-thirds of the net lifted I turned on my flashlight, shined the crew in the boat, and yelled, "Conservation Officer! Hold it right there!" Now in the U.P. when someone is doing something wrong and they hear these famous words they have an almost spontaneous reaction. Run!

Knowing this, the plan was as I yelled out; the other officers would start up the pickup and start dragging the net into shore. Our plan worked great, as far as starting the pickup and pulling the gill net up on shore went. We only had one tactical problem. It seems that there was nothing in the area where the net came over the edge of the boat to catch on. So as we pulled the gill net to shore, the illegal netters kicked their boat into gear and disappeared out into the dark of Lake Michigan.

We did end up with some net and a good theory that did not work out for our night's effort though.

....

We Had Fun

If a person could say one thing about the way things used to be, it would be that we had fun doing our job as game wardens. As the saying goes, "If you didn't laugh at times you would have to sit down and cry."

When I first started out we did not have much of a radio system. We could call the county sheriff department if they had our radio turned on. Other than that you were pretty much on your own out there at night.

At the sheriff department when I started out they did not have a deputy as radio dispatcher. In those days there was this older man that would come down to the jail to sit the radio at night if some of the deputies were out on the road. Needless to say we had no computers and we could not even run a file check without going through another county.

Back in those days you were issued a set of books that had all the vehicle license plate numbers for your county and who they were issued to. If you wanted to know who owned a certain vehicle you just looked it up. But if they were from another county you usually punted.

There was this night we were out working and met up with a couple of deputies. The older man was sitting the radio back at the sheriff department on this night. One of the deputies said, "Watch this." He then took the radio mike and made some strange, spacey sounds into the mike and said in a strange sounding voice, "Tuscola County, Tuscola County, Sputnik One requesting Landing instructions?" There was a dead silence on the other end!

All of a sudden you heard this voice that sounded scared to death, try to whisper over the radio, "Tuscola car 3 did you hear that?" And then dead silence again. I mean the "old fellow" was scared, as we about died laughing.

John Walker Is Forestry Grad

Among those graduating from the Michigan Technological University Forestry Center at Alberta, Mich. recently was John A. Walker, son of Mr. and Mrs. Arthur Walker of Ontonagon.

John graduated with honors, finishing in the top three of his class of 34 members.

He has accepted a position with the Michigan Department of Conservation at Caro, Mich., and he and his wife, Eunice and their son, Johnny, are at home at 135 Hooper St., Caro.

His wife, mother and brothers attended the graduation ceremonies, and also his grandfather, Harry Theiler.

I can honestly say now, "It was last century."

Chapter 18
Life Is Not Always Fair

After you have worked as a game warden for a number of years you soon have to learn to hold in your laughter as people tell you just what they feel is fair and what is not. In this chapter are some short tales that caused them to feel this way.

That Whooshing Is Just Too Hard To Hear!

In the area of the U.P. where I worked as a game warden there are over four hundred lakes. During the winter months there is a lot of ice fishing that takes place on these lakes. First you have to check on the lakes that are closed during the winter months to make sure there is nobody trying to catch fish on them. Then you have to check the fishing activity on the open lakes to see that they are not using to many lines or catching to many fish. Most of the fishermen using these remote lakes travel into them by snowmachine.

The only problem is, if the game warden were to travel into these lakes by snowmobile, and there were illegal fishing activities taking place, they would be corrected long before he got there. The illegal fishermen soon learn to listen for the sound of any snowmobile coming their way. In fact a lot of them get good enough to know the exact sound that the snowmachine the game warden uses makes. So the warden has to come up with a better idea.

One of the officers that worked the area northwest of where I was assigned had a perfect setup. In fact it worked so good that I would hear about how unfair it was to those out on the lake fishing. It seemed that this officer really enjoyed cross-country skiing, so you guessed it. He would take his skies with him and if he wanted to get back to an out of the way lake to check it, he would just put on his skies and off he would go.

You know it is really hard to hear him coming across the snow using this means of transportation. It was totally amazing for me to hear some of those that were caught complaining about the fact that they thought this unfair of the game warden to be doing this.

I was never much of a cross-country skier, but I did make good use of a pair of snowshoes more than once. I can still recall the time another game warden and myself snow shoed into East Lake up off M-94 to catch a whole crew of guys doing some illegal Northern Pike fishing.

We had parked out on M-94 and set off on our shoeshoes. We walked down through the woods so we were about halfway down the lake before we cut through the woods to come up behind the fishermen. We were standing near their warming fire on the ice before they even knew we were there. It is really neat to see the expression of their face when this happens. It sure is hard to hear those whooshes in the snow.

The Legislator Would Never Do That!

Back in the Stone Age when this old fossil started out as a game warden some of the laws you enforced were unreal. I guess the dumbest law that we had to work around was the shining law. You see back then a party could shine all they wanted with a gun right in the car with them as long as it was either broke down or in a case.

This meant that a game warden when he saw someone shining had to get behind him to try to get him to stop. Then the game warden would have to get out of the patrol car, up to the car with the shiners in it, before they could break down a shotgun or pull a bolt out of a bolt-action gun. That's right! All they would have to do is pull the bolt out of a bolt-action firearm before you got to their car to be legal. What a joke this was. There was just no way if the outlaws had their act together you could make this law work.

Finally the legislator in all their wisdom changed the law. They said that if you were shining for deer you could no longer have a firearm that was in the passenger part of a vehicle. This meant you could no longer shine with a firearm in a case or with the bolt in one hand and the rest of the firearm in the other. In may have worked on paper, but it was a joke out in the field where the game warden operated.

We would stop vehicle after vehicle with the shiner sitting in the back seat using the light. You would then have the driver and shooter in the front seats. They would travel along until they spotted a deer, the driver would stop, out would jump the party on the passenger side to run back to the trunk where the key was already in the lock. They would turn the key, open the trunk, and the gun was right there. It did not even have to be in a case if it was carried in the trunk.

During this period if you stopped ten vehicles of shiners that were really after deer, eight would be driving around with a key in the trunk. This too soon became a joke. You went from a firearm being carried in the passenger part of a vehicle to being able to still carry a firearm while shining, only in a trunk with a key in the lock.

Finally the legislator passed a law that basically stated you could not use a light to locate game if you had a means to kill what you were shining anywhere in your vehicle. This meant if you wanted to spot deer to just look at them OK, as long as you left your firearms at home.

I can still remember when word came out that a law like this was being considered in Lansing. A number of the locals that made it a habit to do a little night hunting in the fall could not believe it. I had more than one of them tell me, "They have just gone to far this time!" Another told me, "This is just not fair, they would never pass a law like this, and it would ruin our night hunting." You may not believe this, but honestly there were those poachers out there that really thought it was their right to hunt at night. After all it had been passed down from father to son for generations in some families.

I guess some of the most interesting statements that were said to me by one of the areas most famous night hunter was this, "Well, I guess I will just have to give up my night hunting." He then said, "It will just be cheaper with a lot less risk to put in an order for a deer and let someone else take all the chances."

You can laugh, but there was no doubt in my mind that he was dead serious when he told me this. You see 99% of those caught with illegal deer are caught out in the field while trying to get them. If you had them delivered to your home you sure cut down on your chances of ever being caught with it.

....

Who Are You Again?

I started out as a game warden right at the time they went from a warden driving his personal car to driving a state issued patrol vehicle. There were a lot of advantages to driving one of these state owned patrol cars, but they had one big drawback, it was sure no secret to anyone who you were as you came driving down the road towards them.

It got so the local outlaws seemed to have a radar system to spot a warden's patrol car. Of course those "Exspurts" sitting in the big house had convinced themselves that all the violators that spot a patrol vehicle would just turn over a new leaf and never violate again. If you too believe this would work you would be a prime candidate for some prime swampland with no legal access.

So what did the game warden out in the field have to do, come up with a better idea? If you have read this book you know about the old International pickup we used. It was faded, air force blue. All along one side was remodeled by a few trees. It worked like a charm for driving around checking hunters or fishermen. They never had any idea who you were until it was too late to run.

Then there were the years that we talked our District Supervisor into getting us a Chevy Chevelle to use. You see, back in those days one of the top cars for young people to drive was the 396 version of this car. We never had a 396 model, but we had the next best thing.

To make a good situation even better we were issued a pair of old farmer, striped coveralls back then. We always heard the state got them for free from state prisons where they were made. True? I have no idea. So you would put these on over your uniform and get into your unmarked patrol unit and off you would go.

I can remember stopping this party one time for illegal hunting while on patrol with our unmarked Chevelle. All the time I sat in the patrol car making out the tickets the poacher walked around and around the Chevelle muttering, "Game wardens don't drive a Chevelle, game wardens don't drive a Chevelle..."

Of course there were times when you had to make do with your normal patrol vehicle. One of the biggest problems with a patrol car was the blue light mounted on the roof. Outlaws could spot this on a vehicle long before you ever got within catching distance of them.

So we came up with this idea. We got some car top carriers and mounted a canoe on the roof of a patrol car. When you did this you would not only hide the blue light, but would make the patrol car look a whole lot different as you came down the road. It worked great!

I can recall the time we received a complaint from the MSP post about a drunk driver in the area where we were working. As luck would have it the party came weaving down the road right to us. We stopped him and took him into the post. The sergeant at the post said, "I can just hear it now, the drunk will get into court and say, "But your Honor, I was just driving down the road minding my own business when this canoe pulled up along side my car and pulled me over.''

The judge must not have believed him because we never ended up going to court with this guy.

Those were the days when the object was to catch the bad guys. When this was the case you got to use a few things that made it a littler easier.

....

Team Work

Sometimes there is no rhyme or reason as to why someone gets caught violating. I have told poachers over and over that sometimes I feel that the Good Lord just gets tired of them getting away with it so He gives the game warden a gift.

On this particular evening we had already caught three crews out shining with a firearm along. Needless to say it had been a great night already. We had stopped to get a pop at a little gas station and met a sheriff department patrol unit there.

We all got a pop and decided to park on top of radio tower hill to shoot the breeze for a while and tell the deputies about the crazy crews we had caught already that night. As we sat there a State Police car came up on the hill to join us. We had been there for maybe a half an hour when we observed a car shining on a gravel road a half mile to the south of where we were sitting. We decided to have some fun and made out a game plan.

It was decided that the two patrol cars from the State Police and Sheriff Department would take off down the road to the west, then head south. Then they would go the half-mile south to block the gravel road the shiners were on where it came onto the blacktop road. I was to go west until I hit a gravel road that would cut across to the road the shiner was operating on.

I came up without any lights on behind this car that was shining, until I was just a few feet off his back bumper. Then we turned on the headlights, spotlights and the blue light. All we heard was the car that had been shining wind up and takes off! (It was one of those Super Bees that were made back in those days.) The shiner no sooner got his fast car wound up until his headlights lit up the State Police and Sheriff Department cars that had the road blocked right in front of them. You talk about mad, this guy was livid!

He looked at me and yelled, "You would have never caught me if they hadn't been here!" You know he was right, but sometimes we just get a gift.

Chapter 19
Please, Don't Tell My Wifee

I guess there are always those things that happen when you are too young to really be scared. It is usually sometime later that your brain engages and you realize how lucky you really were that nobody ever got really hurt. Maybe it is just the fact where you thought what you were doing was the most important job in the world and you just had to catch those bad guys no matter what!

Lasting Impression

When this incident took place I was not even a Game Warden yet, but I was still working as a Fire Officer for the old Conservation Department. You have to understand that back in those days the local Fire Officer was assigned to work with the Game Warden during the busy time in the fall of the year. During this time in my career I was working with Lynn most of the time.

On this day we were on patrol in southern Tuscola County working the opening of pheasant season. We had covered a lot of the Southern part of the county, checking a few hunters, but things were really kind of slow. We had just left the little town of Millington when we received a complaint from the sheriff department about some pheasant hunters that were involved in a trespass complaint over east of where we were.

Now you have to understand that usually when a party gets ready to call in a complaint he first tells those that are trespassing that he is going to. It goes something like this, "If you don't get off my property I'm going to call the sheriff department!" Those that are causing the problem usually tell the property owner about this time to "stick it in your ear!" So then being mad the property owner goes into the house and calls in the complaint.

When the officer receives the complaint he already knows that 99% of the time the trespassers are already leaving the area after ticking the farmer off. For this reason the game warden wants to get there as fast as possible to catch them before they have a chance to leave the area. Lynn and I were no different so off we went.

Back then the game wardens were issued a Plymouth 440 patrol car and they would flat fly. I have no idea how fast we were going, but it was a whole lot faster than anyone in his right mind would go over an illegal pheasant complaint. We came flying over the big hill that sits east of Millington doing well over a hundred miles an hour. As we crested this hill we soon had a very serious problem!

You see about a third of the way down this hill, from the crest, there was a gravel road that came onto the main road from the right side. As we came flying over this hilltop and started down a vehicle appeared on the gravel road that did not bother to stop for the stop sign. It just started pulling out onto the blacktop road we were on right in front of us!

This is one of the few times in my career that I cannot recall what or how we managed to miss this car. We came, there it was, and we were sliding by it on our way. The only thing I knew was that I only had enough time to grab the dash and hang on. But we did miss the car and also missed catching the people we had the complaint on.

Later that evening Lynn again picked me up at the house to go out on patrol. As I got into his patrol car I noticed something left from that morning. Back in those days the dash on these cars was a hard plastic covering. Right over the glove box firmly imbedded in the dash were the outlines of both my hands where I had grabbed the dash that morning when I thought we were going to hit that car.

I have tried a number of times since to make a finger marking in this dash material under normal conditions and could not even phase it. It is amazing what you can do when you are scared out of your wits.

....

He Doesn't See Us!

This was one of those nights when I was riding with one of the deputies for the Tuscola County Sheriff Department. Back in those days the game wardens used to spend a lot of time working with the local sheriff department. There were really two reasons for this, the first was we could only drive a limited number of miles each month, the other reason was the fact that most deputies were local people so they knew the area you were assigned too. You soon found out you could learn a lot about the area and the local outlaws by working with these men. Also back then most of our radios were connected with the local sheriff department when our office was closed.

On this even I was riding with a deputy working the areas of the "Thumb" near Cass City. We had spent a few hours working an area called the Deford State Game Area for shiners without any luck. It was now about 2:30 in the morning so we decided to head back into the office.

We had just made our way toward Cass City when we received a call that one of the police officers in a small town right near the Tuscola-Huron County line was involved in a shootout. The deputy driving headed up north about as fast as he could go.

Now remember that back in this period patrol cars were made to move. It was before all of Ralph Nader's junk got on them. This patrol car was a 454 Oldsmobile. We came up to an intersection north of Cass City and turned to the west and the deputy opened it up once again. He had both the overhead lights and the sirens going as we headed toward the area of the complaint.

We had passed a couple of cars when we came up on this other car traveling the same way we were. At this point we were going well over a hundred and twenty miles an hour when the deputy got in the left-hand lane to pass this car. To this day I don't know why I had this feeling, but all of a sudden I yelled to the driver, "Bill! He's going to take a left!" The driver of this car did not have a blinker on.

Unless you have been there, you have no idea how fast a patrol car will come up on a vehicle slowing to make a left hand turn in front of you. You also have no idea how big that car looks as you think you are about to hit it!

This vehicle did turn left right in front of us, but we managed to get our patrol car back in the right hand lane enough to miss it. But please don't ask me how. I don't think that the party driving this car ever really knew we were there.

The funny thing is how many times you just had that feeling for no reason that ended up getting you out of a serious problem. There is no doubt at that speed we would have all went to that perfect deer blind in the sky.

....

Not Another Deputy!

This is just a short tale that has a two-part warning that most people seem to not understand.

On this patrol I was riding once again with a deputy on night patrol. We were working an area where there were a lot of deer, but you have to understand that the deputy's main job was still to handle any complaints that came along.

After we had ridden around for half the night the deputy received a call about a family problem that another law enforcement agency needed some help with right away. Off we went.

We were on a state highway that comes into this little town where there is a five-way intersection. The way we came in we not only had the right-of-way, but once again we were running with the overhead lights and siren on. As we came into this intersection from the east at a pretty good clip, I saw a car coming into the intersection from our left. I said, "Jim! He doesn't know we're here!"

Here we come in the middle of the night like a flying Christmas tree with red and blue lights flashing, a siren whaling, and all the other lights on the patrol car on, how could he not see us! But he didn't and pulled right into the intersection right in front of us!

But thank goodness, we had slowed down enough when I yelled so we missed him. But what did we notice about this car! The party driving it must have got up in the early morning to go to work and only scraped a little 4x4 opening on his windshield to look out. All the rest of the windshield and both side windows were still covered with a heavy frost. I have to wonder how many people do this on frosty mornings?

The other thing you soon learn is that if a person has all the windows up in the car with the radio going they will not hear the sirens from a patrol car no matter how loud you think it is. Put on top of this the time it takes the normal person to react when they do hear the siren and usually the patrol car will be by them.

It Can Even Happen On The Water

On this beautiful Saturday I was out on boat patrol with a Marine Deputy from the county sheriff department. They had a lot bigger and nicer boat than we had at that time for working out on the big lake so we would team up together a lot on weekends.

You also have to remember that back when this old fossil started out as a game warden we did not enforce marine safety laws! In those days the enforcement of these laws was the responsibility of the county sheriff department, not the conservation officers. So when we were on patrol the deputy would write any tickets that were written for marine law violations and I would enforce the hunting or fishing law violations we came across. That was the way things were done back in the "Good Old Days".

On this weekend afternoon I was out on patrol on Saginaw Bay with the Marine Deputy from the Tuscola County Sheriff Department. The Marine Deputy was my next-door neighbor so we worked a lot together. The way the system worked back then, he would check the boaters for marine violations and I would check fishermen for fish law violations. It worked out real well and we spent a good number of weekends during the summer working together.

During this particular afternoon we had been out on the bay only a couple of hours and had planned to work up until suppertime. After checking a number of boats it seemed like there were very few boats left out on the bay to check. We took a ride along the shore over to the Fish Point area when the deputy said, "I think we had better head back in."

It was kind of abnormal because it was a beautiful afternoon with the sun shining and there should be some boaters and fishermen coming out on the bay for evening activity. But he felt we should pack up and head in so we did.

We loaded the patrol boat on the trailer and headed back toward Caro where his office was. We were only about halfway back when all of a sudden the sky turned pitch black, it began to pour, and then big, huge, hailstones started bouncing off the patrol car! I mean it was so bad we had to pull over and stop. It was so bad we thought it would wreck the boat behind us, but there were two officers that were sure glad that the little voice had told the marine deputy that he had better get off the bay.

After it let up we continued back toward Caro, but now we were following a 2-track trail down the middle of the road the hail was so deep on the blacktop. In fact when I got home wifee told me she was so scared it was going to take the windows out of the house, she had the kids lay in the middle of the floor with a blanket over them.

But once again that Guardian Angel that follows Game Wardens around came through, even if he had to contact the Marine Deputy to do it.

Chapter 20
The Tales About Wolves

Well, I came across something interesting the other day. I was reading some old Michigan Conservation Department Magazines from 1937 and 1938. In these magazines I came across a couple of articles that really caught my interest. With the idea of getting everything back to the way it was in the good old days the DNR brought wolves into the U.P. to replant them. Now according to the Exspurts there is nothing to worry about. They tell us that some of the old tales we hear are just not true. But the following are articles printed in the official magazine of these same Exspurts that just may tell us a different side of the story.

Page 11 of the Michigan Conservation dated June 1938. Memories of Killer Wolves (Killing for fun) W.J. Pearson, the state's first chief fire warden, and J. A. Vizena of Munising, a former warden and now land examiner in the upper peninsula, learned something about the viciousness of wolves on a snowshoe trip several years ago.

Pearson was swinging through the Upper Peninsula perfecting his fire organization and stopped to visit Vizena. The latter invited him to make a little inspection trip into an area where he believed a pack of wolves was running deer. The wolves had been seen only a day or two before.

The two men fastened on their snowshoes and started out on a fairly long trek over the crust. After a time they came upon tracks, which confirmed the reports made to Vizena that a fairly large pack of wolves had invaded the territory.

A little farther along they found the carcass of a deer. It had been ripped open along one side, almost from shoulder to flank, but no part of it had been eaten. Soon they saw another carcass in a similar state, and then another and another.

Before they turned homeward, Pearson and Vizena counted 26 mutilated deer several of which were still breathing. In none of the attacks had the wolves shown any disposition to eat what they had brought down. They obviously had been indulging in a carinate orgy of sport.

August 1938 on page ten of the Michigan Conservation magazine. Memories: Beef for wolves this story of a man chased by a pack of wolves will be in next weeks Fish Report.

But as I read these two stories I could not help but recall a statement made by a college president years ago. He said, "One thing you can be sure of is this, humans never learn from history." "As the wheel of life comes around once again, they end up making the same mistakes, they never learned from what happened years before."

Now the Michigan Conservation Department (now the DNR) must have felt there was some truth to these stories or they never would have printed them in their official department magazine. The Exspurts of today after all are a lot smarter than those that lived back in the 30's, right? Personally, I have to wonder at times or is the college president I heard right?

....

Well, on a lighter note here is another wolf story from 1938.

Memories:

Beef For The Wolves

No one knows how many furious debates have raged over the question of whether wolves will attack humans, but the subject has long been a common battleground for both veterans and tenderfeet.

No matter how many scoffed at the idea of the wolf working up enough courage to engage a man in combat there always were others who claimed to know of actual instances. Now, with the wolf extremely scarce in Michigan, it is necessary to tap the store of experiences in the past to argue the question.

One of those whose span extends back to the days when it was nothing extraordinary to see timber wolves in Michigan is Joe Decoto, 56-year-old Indian living in the vicinity of L'anse in the upper peninsula. Joe began to trap and hunt when he was scarcely more than a papoose and made his living that way until about 15 years ago when he found it more profitable to serve as a guide.

Joe tells of an incident, which happened before the automobile had come along to shrink distance and time. Getting supplies for lumber camps then meant something of a journey and it was on one of these trips that a lumberjack suddenly became aware that he was being pursued by wolves.

The lumberjack had been to town and was on his way back to camp with a load of beef quarters and other provisions on his bobsled. He was alone without a gun.

The wolves kept drawing closer and closer to the bobsled. The winter had been long and severe and the animals were obviously half starved. There were seven of them in the pack. The lumberjack whipped his horses but the wolves came on until the leader was within a few feet of the back of the bobsled. He was an ugly, fang-showing brute who exhibited no fear.

The man realized that he could not temporize with the situation much longer. He couldn't get away and yet he didn't see much chance for himself and his horses in staying to do battle with the hungry animals.

Desperate for some kind of a plan, he suddenly thought of the quarters of beef on the bobsled. Quickly he pulled one out and tossed it off the rear end. The wolves pounced upon it, growling ferociously and fighting among themselves while tearing off huge chunks of meat.

The lumberjack's relief was short. It lasted no longer than the beef that was gobbled up in a minute. Their appetites apparently only whetted, the wolves resumed the chase and soon were stalking the bobsled again, even more boldly them before.

The lumberjack tossed off another quarter of beef. And another, and another, all the time belaboring his horses to the limit of their speed. The wolves would pause each time only long enough to devour the hunk of meat, which seemed, the lumberjack said afterwards, to require not more then a few seconds, and then come on again.

The beef lasted just long enough for the man to reach the safety of the camp. There wasn't a strip of beef left by the time he arrived.

It was a thrilling account. Perhaps the lumberjack made it too thrilling. A quiet investigation was begun and the next day all of the beef quarters were found at his shanty. And that may be what Joe thinks about the contention that wolves will attack a man.

....

The Good Old Days?

One thing I did find of interest in one of these magazines was an article where six fishermen were caught with 74 undersize brook trout in their possession. The offenders were arraigned in court and convicted. They were fined a total of $2,965. Can you believe this?

Back when you could purchase a new car for around $400. My Dad bought a home a few years later for $250. (That was a two stories, three-bedroom home.) Yet for some fishermen to receive a penalty $2,965! If this penalty was to have been increased at the rate of everything else since that date to this, could we even figure out what it would cost you to violate under the same circumstances today?

I came across a letter the other day that I thought might be of interest to some of you. We all think that the fines are "big" for violators of conservation laws today, but this is not true. Really back in the twenties and thirties the party that got caught paid more than a person does today. If you throw in what a person, even one that does not work, makes today we have really not kept up in our fines and cost. But where we really lost it is the fact that we seem scared to take away the equipment that they used to violate with in this day and age. When is the last time a party around here lost their car for having a couple of illegal deer in it? They did back in 1933!!

From 1929 to 1939 there was an average of 200 rifles and 300 shotguns confiscated. From 1964 through 1974 the annual average was 40 rifles and 25 shotguns confiscated. This figure has never climbed back where it was in the thirties. In 1936 there were 1,542 traps confiscated. In 1932, 106 spears and in 1935, 168 spears were condemned.

GET THIS!! IN 1933 THERE WERE TEN (10) CARS CONFISCAT-ED. IN 1931 THERE WERE TWENTY-SEVEN (27) BOATS TAKEN.

In 1938, we confiscated 8-snares, 729-Christmas trees. In 1932, 5-ferrets, 3-bird cages. In 1933,   7-ferrets and 3-dogs. In 1936, 54-cedar posts, 7-bushels of mussels, 10-logs, 238-pounds of clam shells, 10-cord of spruce pulp and 81-Christmas Trees. In 1934-35, 1-cross cut saw, 1-weasel, 2-bags of mussels, 421-Norway logs, 1-tent, 4000 feet of swamp timber, 50-minnow traps, 20-cord of white birch and one dog.

All these items were on top of the normal things confiscated by people caught during the years listed. If you compare the average fine and cost from the twenties and thirties, with the average fine and cost from the seventies going into the eighties, you would find they were within $10.00 of each other. Now I ask you, " Would ten to fifteen dollars, the average fine in 1927, buy more than $12.54, the average fine in 1974 in there respective years? Is it any wonder that outlaws do not have any respect for the conservation laws in this day and age?

Dear Friend,

I guess there is no way that I deserve all the blessings I have received in my life. God has been so good to me. I listened to my Dad while growing up and ended up with the job I always wanted since my high school days. While in the army I met and married my wife and God blessed us with four wonderful children. Now we have six grand-children. I could go on and on talking about the blessings of God, but there is some-thing more important I would like to tell you about. While in the army a friend gave me a book titled 'The Greatest Story Ever Told'. I read this book and it really got me thinking. Later I read the book called 'What would Jesus do?' From these two books I started to wonder about Jesus dying on the cross once for all and I realized that all included me. After meeting my wife I asked the Lord to forgive my sins and come into my heart, but there was always a little question in my heart about being saved. A cou-ple of years later I attended some special meetings being preached by a bear hunting friend of mine Evangelist Pete Rice. During these meetings I made sure about my sal-vation and have never had this doubt in my heart again.

Once I heard Brother Pete preach on John 3:16 'For God so loved the world that he gave his only begotten son, that whosoever believeth in Him should not perish, but have everlasting life'. At the end of his preaching six people walked the isle to get saved. One was a tough, old, trapper that I knew and it really impressed me. What does being saved mean? It simply means that one understands that Jesus came and died on the cross for our sins, that we understand we are a sinner, and we ask Jesus to come into our heart, forgive our sins, and be our Savior.

You can use what is called the Romans Road to help you with this. It is as easy as dri-ving down a 2-track out in the woods. If you would take a Bible you would find these verses. Romans 3:23 "All have sinned and come short of the glory of God." This means that all people have sinned and need to realize it. Romans 6:23 states, "the wages of sin is death". This means if we do not ask forgiveness of God for our sins we will die with payment due for them. I Corinthians 15:3 says, "Christ died for our sins". This means payment has already been paid in full for our sins by Jesus death on the cross. Romans 6:23 tells us, "the gift of God is eternal life through Jesus Christ our Lord". Everything that has to be done has been done, but for our part. Romans 10:13 tells us how, "Whosoever shall call upon the name of the Lord shall be saved". This means all a person has to do is understand they are a sinner, that Jesus died on the cross for them, and ask Him to come into their heart and forgive their sins. Then you like so many before you will have everlasting life to look forward to.

I pray you will do this and someday I will see you in heaven and you can tell me about it.

Chapter 21
A Yooper Vacation

One of the things that writing my books has caused is all the calls and requests I get asking about taking a vacation in Michigan's U.P. There are a few things that if you are making a circle of the U.P. you won't want to miss. So I thought, if I get this many request maybe I should put a few pointers in my new book.

First of all let me say that a person on vacation has a perfect circle to make in exploring the U.P. using both US-2 and M-28. In setting up our trip we will start on US-2 at the Mackinaw Bridge and go west.

First of all remember all the neat things about St. Ignace. You can stop at the **Big Boy Restaurant** right on US-2 to set up a game plan. You have **Mackinaw Island** right there off St. Ignace. One thing you will not want to miss before you leave here is the **Deer Ranch** right on US-2 going west. This stop is a must for you and your family to start things off right.

As you are going west on US-2 you will come to Brevort a little town with **Gustafson's Smoked Fish**. A stop here is a must if you want to get a taste of a real U.P. treat. Their smoked fish and jerky are super. I have shipped gift packages of their jerky all over the country.

As you continue west you will come to another little town called Epoufette. Here you will find the **Skyline Restaurant**, which I feel has the best view of any restaurant in the U.P.

The next place that I feel is worth your stop is **GarLyn Farm**. Here you will get to see everything from bear to wolves as you tour a wild animal farm.

Right down the road you will come to Naubinway with **King's Store**. This store and gift shop has a little bit of everything for you to look over.

You can always go off US-2 too little towns like Curtis, which has a number of nice lakes around it. But as you continue along you will come to the little town of Gulliver. Here you have a great place to check out called **Seul Choix Point Lighthouse**.

Now you have arrived where I live in Manistique. Here you have **Sunny Shores, Big Boy**, or **Hardee's** Restaurants to stop at for a break. **Lakeshore shell** also has some nice clean gas stations if you need to fuel up. Downtown Manistique has the **Mustard Seed Gift Shop** along with **Top-O-Lakes Sports and Gifts**. In the Manistique area you have **Big Springs State Park (Kitch-iti-kipi)** and the Indian Lake area to check out. There is some fine fishing in this area with a number of good resorts to stay at.

We are now at Garden Corners on Bay-De-Noc where you have **Foxy's Den** for gas and tourist information. Here too **Tyelene's Restaurant**, which now has one of the best Friday night fish fries in the area. From here you can go down on the Garden Peninsula to see Fayette State Park.

In Rapid River you have **Jack's Family Restaurant** where you sure get your moneys worth.

In the Escanaba-Gladestone area there are a number of fine eating-places. You have **Delona's** and the **Drifters Restaurants**. Both of these serve food the old fashion way. As you travel around the U.P. remember along with trying some smoked fish you must try some good pasties. They are a must here in God's country.

Remember US-2 goes all the way from east to west across the U.P. All the way from the Mackinaw Bridge to Ironwood. Any time you can take a number of roads that cut up to M-28. But as you do you will want to check out the **Bond Falls** area. Remember that Upper Michigan is known for some of the finest waterfalls in the Midwest.

Some of the things you will not want to miss seeing along M-28 now going from the west back toward the east and the Mackinaw Bridge are:

One of the first things you will want to see is the **Porcupine Mountains** area with Lake of the Clouds. This is in the Ontonagon area along Lake Superior, which has some great agate picking along the shore. When you get into Ontonagon you will want to stop by the **Ontonagon Historical Museum**. In my unbiased, predigest opinion this is one of the finest museums you will ever come across in all your travels anywhere.

When you leave the Ontonagon area you will travel over to the Copper Country and the Keweenaw Peninsula area going up to Copper Harbor. There are enough places to stop up here to spend a full day. **Copper World Gift Shop** in Calumet is a good place to check out.

Later your trip will take you around Keweenaw Bay to the L'anse and Baraga area. Here you will want to stop at the **Hilltop Restaurant** going west out of L'anse. This restaurant is famous for it's big sweet rolls and has been for years. This stop was always a must when traveling through the area with my Mom.

As you continue along you will come to the intersection of M-28 and M-95 corner where you have a little restaurant that is one of the best places to eat between Marquette and L'anse. Just a few miles down the road you will come to **"The Yoopers Tourist Trap"**. If you need a good laugh after all your travels here is a good place to stop.

Right down the road on your way to Marquette you will see the **National Ski Museum**. Then going into Marquette you will have to look for **A Touch of Finland** right across from the Westwood Mall. In Marquette you have the gift shop at the **Marquette Monthly Magazine**. There is also a nice **Marquette Museum** that is worth some of your time.

Around the lake from Marquette you will come to the little town of Munising, here you can spend some time. They have **Pictured Rocks National Park**. You can take a boat trip on one of the **Pictured Rock Cruises** boats out of Munising. When you get ready to eat you will find the **Dog Patch Restaurant** and gift shop waiting for you. This place is talked about all over the state. Right next to the Dog Patch you will see a gift shop called the **Gift Station**. You have to stop here and see their collection of clocks and extra fine gifts. I always have to stop here with my daughter to check out the Snowbabies as we travel thru Munising. Before you leave you may want to gas up at the Shell Station that is always nice and clean.

Right after you cross the famous Seney Stretch into Seney you will see M-77 going up to Grand Mara's on Lake Superior. Here on the bay you will find **Welker's Restaurant and Resort** waiting for you.

Back in Seney there is the **Golden Grill Restaurant** run by a Mennonite family that is famous for its food.

Now as we go along M-28 we come to the road going down into Curtis, which has the three beautiful lakes with some fine fishing. On the corner where you turn toward Curtis you will see the **Triangle Restaurant**.

Now we are going into the big town of Newberry. Right across from the school is a gift shop with an old fashion ice cream bar called **Country Gallery Gifts**. They also have a larger gift store down town. As you leave Newberry going north some of the best times on your whole trip around the U.P. are before you.

The first place you <u>must</u> stop is **Oswald's Bear Ranch**! Of all the places you plan to see in your travels across Yooper Land this place is a must. You will never see anything like this anywhere else. In fact if the truth was known you will never meet anyone like Dean Oswald anywhere else in all your travels.

Now we are into the area of the **Tahquamenon Falls**. Of all the waterfalls in the U.P. these two, the Upper and Lower Tehquamenon Falls are maybe the best known. At the Upper Falls you have the **Camp Nineteen Gift Shop** that is just a beautiful place to stop. There is also a nice gift shop at the Lower Falls.

In the little town of Paradise you will find some quaint little gift and antique shops. After leaving Paradise you can travel along Lake Superior to the Soo and back to the Mackinaw Bridge.

Remember the U.P. is a great place to live and an excellent place to visit.

These are just a few places that you can check out in your travels, but just remember there is much, much more worth looking at here in God's Country.

I will close with this story. There was this police officer on vacation with his family going north in Michigan with plans to visit Canada. Just before the Mackinaw Bridge he stopped at a State Police Post and asked the sergeant sitting desk if he could lock up his service revolver seeing he was planning on going into Canada and could not take it with him. The sergeant said OK, so off went our Detroit Police Officer with his family to visit Canada.

As things would have it when this Detroit Police Officer stopped back at the post to pick up his service revolver the same sergeant was sitting desk. As he was getting him his revolver he asked the officer how he enjoyed Canada? The Detroit officer replied, "We just loved it!" The sergeant then ask him where they had went? Once again the Detroit police officer replied, "O" first we went across the bridge to the Soo. Then we went to Brimley, Paradise, White Fish Point, and over to Grand Mara's. It was just beautiful and we had a great time."

The sergeant said he just looked at him, and didn't have the heart to tell him he never made it to Canada and in fact had never even left Michigan, seeing he had such a great vacation! So our Detroit Police Officer left still thinking he had a great Canadian vacation.

Bethel Baptist Church
118 East Elk St
Manistique, MI 49854

Dear Friends;

Thank you for your interest in the Bethel Baptist Scholarship Fund. The Scholarship Fund was started by Retired Game Warden John Walker as a way of assisting Christian young people going to Bible College. There are many scholarships available for secular colleges, but very few available for Bible Colleges.

To date, the Scholarship Fund has been able to assist 12 students going to a variety of Christian Colleges. The total funds given to date (as of the Spring Semester of 2000) to help young people are $12,500. Three young people have finished four years of college with the help of the Scholarship Fund. There are currently four students being assisted at this time.

Current assets of the Scholarship Fund are located at North County Bank. $10,483.54 is being held in CD's. The remaining $11,661 is deposited in an interest bearing checking account. The goal of the Fund is to be able to help more students in the future, to grow the assets until the interest is able to cover the scholarships, and possibly increase the amount of the scholarships.

As we look back over the life of the Scholarship Fund, it is truly wonderful to see what God has done to enable us to assist young people going to Christian Colleges. The total amount of the fund God has blessed us with is $34,644.54. Much of the funds have come from the sales of Sgt. Walker's books.

Thank you once again for your interest in the Bethel Baptist Scholarship Fund. Please Pray with us as we seek God's direction and blessings for the future.

In Christ's Love,
Pastor Joseph Crowder

Glossary Backwoods

Up here in the Great North Woods, there is a tendency to use terms or phrases to make a point. To some of you, they may be used in a way you never realized they could be. Other words or terms, you may just have not had the opportunity to ever use. This Backwoods Glossary is to help you out in understanding why we talk like we do.

U.P. (Upper Michigan): If, for some strange reason, you have never traveled in Michigan, these two letters would seem strange to you. First, understand that Michigan has two peninsulas the upper and lower. The Lower Peninsula is made up of two parts, Lower Michigan and Northern Michigan. But, the really important part of Michigan lies across the Mackinaw Bridge. This part of Michigan is called the U.P., for the Upper Peninsula of Michigan. The people up here in the U.P. live in their own little world and like it that way. The only problem is that most of the laws are passed down in Lower Michigan to correct their problems, and then they affect us, who may not even be part of that problem. Some of the Big City folks that pass these laws never have learned to understand and love the U.P. like we that live here do. The natives of the U.P. have trouble understanding the "why-for" about some of these laws; therefore they feel they really must not apply to them.

Two of the biggest industries in the U.P. are paper mills and the men that work in the woods supplying trees to these mills so they can produce their product. There are probably more colleges in the U.P., per capita, than anywhere else in the country. But even with this, there are still a lot of natives up here that feel you could sure ruin a good person if you sent them to one of these colleges. News of a serious crime will travel from one side of the U.P. to the other like a wild fire. Because most people up here are not used to it. To them, serious crimes are when someone takes a deer or some fish illegally and is dumb enough to get caught. They don't even take these crimes to seriously unless the poacher should step over the line and get to greedy.

Sports teams that play teams from other towns in the U.P. always seem to have relatives, or friends, on the other team. Everyone knows someone, or someone that married someone, that knew someone from over there. To win a state championship, you have to beat those teams from "down state". To do this is a dream come true for any red-blooded U.P. boy or girl.

When I was growing up, we had only had part-time radios. So we had to be Green Bay (Wisconsin) Packer and Milwaukee Brave fans. As a boy living in the Western U.P., we could not pick up any radio stations that carried broadcast of the teams from Lower Michigan. For this reason, we grew up feeling that we were a state unto ourselves. We could not be part of Lower Michigan, because it was just to far away, and the only way to get there was by boat. We knew we were not part of Wisconsin, so we were just the Good Old U.P.!

Up here in the U.P., where life is tough, but things are good, and it is just a great place to live.

Some backwoods (U.P.) terms:

2-TRACK:(roads) The U.P. has hundreds of miles of this type of roads. All these roads consist of are two tire ruts worn into the ground from all the vehicle travel throughout the years. Usually you have a high, grass-covered center and mud holes in the low spots. This is one of the reasons that so many people in the U.P. feel you cannot live without a 4x4 pickup. These roads are never worked on or improved and you get what you see.

Blacktop Roads: These are the 2-tracks, which are worse than unimproved roads. They are covered by mud or clay and it is a real trick to stay between the trees on some of these. There are also a lot of these type roads for which the U.P. is famous. Many a fishermen or hunter has spent hours and hours trying to get out of one of these blacktop roads, usually after you misjudged what you were getting into. Two of the first things I learned after becoming a Game Warden stationed in the U.P. were: It's hard to get 2-ton stuck at fifty miles an hour, so wind it up and keep moving. The other one follows point one, you are never really stuck till you stop. In other words, if one of these blacktop areas sneaks up on you, floor it and don't stop 'til you reach high ground or hit something unmoveable.
Poachers: These are not people that cook eggs in hot water, but may get

themselves in hot water now and then. They are outlaws that rob the honest hunters and fishermen of their chance to get game and fish legally. In years past, it was a way of life in the U.P. that was passed down from generation to generation. When it was an accepted thing to do, the Game Warden not only had a hard time catching the poachers, but he usually had an even harder time trying to get a conviction in the local courts.

Shining: (Shinning, Shining, Shiners), Shiners are the poachers that use a spotlight to look for deer at night, in order to shoot them. Until the fines got to high, it was the way that a lot of the outlaws did their hunting here in the U.P. They would take a pair of spotlights, hook them up in their vehicle, and then drive around while casting the rays of the spotlights out into fields or an old orchard, until they spotted a deer. The deer, blinded by the bright light, would stand there staring at the light while the poacher got out his gun and shot it. There is really no sport in it, because it is so deadly. You will notice I spelled shinning, with two "n's" at times. Well, I did this on my tickets for dozens of cases throughout the years; until a State Trooper told me it was spelled wrong. He said it should only have one "n", so on the next couple tickets I changed how I spelled shining. You see for years, when I caught someone hunting deer at night with a spotlight, the only thing I would write for a charge on the ticket was the one word "shinning". With the one word spelled, Shinning, they knew what they did, I knew what they had done, and most important the average U.P. Judge knew what they were standing before him for doing. Well, the first time I caught a crew out spotlighting for deer and put shining (with one n) on their ticket they pled "Not Guilty". The spelling must have confused them and so was I.

Spearers: These are people that have a way of taking fish with the use of a spear. The spear can have from three to five prongs, with pointed tips; these prongs have barbs on the end to hold the fish on the spear after they spear it. Now in some areas, it is legal to spear certain types of non-game fish. The problem the Game Warden has is with those that spear trout, salmon, walleye, etc. or "game fish". When these fish come into real shallow water to spawn, a Game Warden will spend hour after hour watching the fish spawning in these areas.

Extractors: This is a term for those illegal fishermen that may come along a creek with a spear trying to extract the spawning fish from the creek. They may use other devices besides a spear. For insurance, a weighted hook, hand nets, their hands, etc.

Gill Netters: These are people, both legal and illegal, that use a gill net to take fish. In some areas, there is a commercial fishery allowed with the use of gill nets, but in Michigan it is never legal for "sport" fishermen to use a gill net to take fish. A gill net is made up of nylon string in little squares (it looks something like a small woven wire fence) built so the fish will swim into the net putting their head through the square openings. Then, they get caught when their larger body will not fit through the squares and their gills keep them from backing out of the nets. I have observed illegal gill net fishermen take hundreds of pounds of steelhead in a couple of hours, if they set their gill nets in the right spot.

Fish house or fish shed: In areas of the U.P., along the great lakes where there is a legal commercial fishery, most of those businesses involved have a building where they clean, box in ice, and store their catch. They may also repair their nets in this building. On account of the smell around a full time commercial fishing operation, most of these sheds are located away from any residence. They also may be on the riverbank where the commercial fisherman ties up his fish tug. For this reason they are often used for illegal activity, sometimes by others than those that own them.

Deer camp: A deer camp can be any type of building used for offering protection from the elements. It is also used as a "get-a-way from home during the hunting season. Some are as nice as any house, better than some, while others may be made out of plastic, heavy paper, scrap lumber, or anything to keep the weather out. The following rules are some of the usual type that are proper for deer camp life.

(1) You cannot shave or take a bath, no matter how many days you may be staying at camp. You are allowed to wash your face and hands. But this is your own choice; you do not have to if you do not want to. This is one reason young boys love to go to deer camp with Dad.

(2) There is no proper way to dress while at deer camp, if it feels good wear it! You can even wear the same clothes all week long. This includes

your socks, if you can catch them after the first three days at camp.

(3) The "menu" is always made up of all the "proper" things that you cannot afford to eat all the rest of the year at home. Both good and bad for you.

(4) It is never wrong to tell a "true" story on another camp member. Remembering it is of more value if you can dress it up a little to make him suffer all the time you are telling it. During the telling of his misfortune we must all remember that we will all pay for our mistakes, sooner or later, if and when our hunting "buddies" find out about them.

(5) It is a crime, punishable by banishment, to talk about school, or schoolwork, or any work for that matter while at deer camp.

(6) You can throw, hang or just leave your socks and clothes anywhere they land when you remove them. You can hang your wet socks on anything that has something to hang them from to try and dry them out before the next days hunt. Always remembering it is "most" important to have dry socks by daybreak the next morning.

(7) What may be called work at home is not work at deer camp. Therefore getting things done at deer camp is not classified as work, but a team effort. For this reason, it is not wrong for a boy to do dishes, sweep a floor, pick up trash (that he missed getting in the trash can when he threw it that way, with one of his famous hook shots), or even do what Dad asks him to do, the first time Dad asks him to do it.

You would have to spend a week at a real U.P. deer camp to really know the true feeling of being a U.P. deer hunter. With these easy-to-apply rules, you can see why deer camp life is so important to a boy during his informative teenage years. It is really important that a young man start out with a proper perspective on life.

Big House: This is the Michigan State Capital; from some areas of the U.P. it can be over 400 miles away. In Lansing, this is where "they" compile all the rules and ideas that are put out to confuse the average hunter or fisherman, while out in the field. It is the feeling of a lot of U.P. sportsmen, that most of those that work down there, in Lansing's Big House, never in their lives set foot in the real out-of-doors, or wet a fishing line in a back woods stream. What they know, they got from someone that wrote a book without ever having set their feet in a real woods, or having gone backwoods fishing either. It is just passed on from desk to desk, year after year, put into volumes of rules and law books that we out in the field have to learn to live with. This while trying to enjoy ourselves out in the real Northwood's, Michigan's U.P.

Wifee: (W-IF-EE; wify) this is one's wife. To pronounce it right, you say the "W" sound, then the "IF", than draw out the "EE".

Big Lake: This can be any of the Great Lakes that border Michigan. Instead of saying, " I went fishing out on Lake Michigan Saturday". A native from the U.P. would say, "I went fishing on the Big Lake Saturday afternoon".

Off-road vehicles: ATV'S, ORV'S, dirt bikes, etc. These may be any of the type vehicles that are made primarily to operate off an improved road. Some may be homemade, while others are sold by dealers. In the U.P. you will find a lot of these used by sportsmen to get around when hunting and fishing.

Game Wardens: Conservation Officer, C.O.'s, and Game Wardens are all one and the same, up here in the U.P. They have been around for better than 100 years serving the people of Michigan. The stories they can tell and those told on them are told over and over around the U.P. This is how my newspaper, story telling got started.

Holiday Stations: Holiday? Here, in Michigan's U.P., you always hear the expression, "I'm going to stop by Holiday on the way". Some of you folks may not understand what a Holiday is and how far advanced the U.P. is over other areas of our country. I'll try to explain. Holiday, here in the north country is a gas station-store. The Holiday Stations have been around for years and years, and in the U.P. they are like a mini-mall. The U.P. and Holiday were way ahead of the rest of the world on this idea of doing all your shopping in one stop. Get your gas plus whatever else you may need here at the Holiday. Sometimes it just takes awhile for you all to catch up to us, Yoopers.

Years ago when Christmas time came around, you went down to the Holiday. Here you did all your Christmas shopping. It had a great toy selection, in fact, in most U.P. towns the best to be found. If company dropped in for a surprise visit and you needed food items, off you went to the Holiday to get what you needed. When hunting and fishing season rolled around, they put out a paper and sales ad to get you into the Holiday to fill your needs, everything from guns and ammo, to poles, hooks, and line. If you snagged your waders, off you went to the Holiday for new ones. If your feet got cold out deer hunting, off to the Holiday for warm footgear you went. If your motorized deer blind broke down on a weekend, off to the auto parts section of the Holiday to get what you needed. What am I saying? Before the rest of the world was smart enough to think about putting other than gas and oil supplies in their gas stations the Holiday was there. Now they have moved up one more step because most Holiday Stations have copies of my books for sale.

Remember when traveling through the U.P., if a town does not have a Holiday station, keep on trucking till you find one because that town you are in has not arrived yet!

Copper Country: In so many parts of my book, you will read about things that took place in the Copper Country. This area covers what is called the Keweenaw Peninsula over to the area of the copper mines to the west. Those of us that lived in the Copper Country felt you were going into the world of the great unknown if you left Ontonagon, Houghton, Baraga, or Keweenaw County. In fact, a person growing up when I did may have left the Copper Country for the first time when he went into the service. The Copper Country is really a melting pot of people from all over the world. When I was growing up, it was nothing for some of the old folks not being able to speak English; they talked in their native language. In fact, one of the things that really bugged a teenage boy from the Copper Country was when there were a couple of girls your buddy and you wanted to get to know, and they would talk back and forth in Finnish, and we did not have the foggiest idea what they were saying. The history of the Copper Country is both interesting and unreal if you study it. A person could move away and be gone for years, but when asked where they are from, they always answer the Copper Country.

In the Copper Country, everybody knows somebody that knows somebody else. When on a radio show talking about my first book, "A Deer Gets Revenge", a party called in and wanted to know if I was Harry Theiler's grandson. Then another party called in and wanted to know if I was Tim Walker's brother. (Tim is my brother that lives in a home in Hancock, MI, in the Copper Country). Copper Country people are special people that help make up a place called the U.P. where people know and care about each other. Come visit the U.P. and Copper Country someday, and you will see what I mean.

The other day: I keep telling my kids and the readers of my newspaper article that when I use the saying, "The other day", it could mean anytime between birth and death. It is up to the person you are talking too, to try and figure out what era you are talking about. Up here in the U.P., a party could start to tell you a hunting story by saying, " The other day a buddy and I...." and the story may have taken place back in the forties. (1940's) You have to remember that good stories never really get old; they just get better and added to in the telling of them. There was one officer I worked with could he tell stories! He would get going into a story and you would sit there and listen. Pretty soon bits and pieces would start to ring a bell. Then all of a sudden it would dawn on you that you were with him when "his story" took place, but you really never remembered it happening like he was telling it, or could it have? One of my boys called me from college a while back (another one of those times that means nothing in U.P. phrases) to ask me about the history of the 60's. This was for a paper he had to do for a history course. I told him, "Son, the 60's do not qualify as history yet. That is when your dad says, you know the other day, or awhile back, and that makes it today not history."

Exspurt: Sometimes in the U.P. we have our own way of spelling and understanding things. Here is one of those terms. I have a buddy that is a U.P. potato farmer. (You have to really wonder about anybody that tries to farm in the U.P.) But this buddy has a great definition for all those exspurts that rule down in the Big House. It is one of those terms you have to think about, but the more you think about it, the more you feel that this potato farmer may go down in history as a great U.P. philosopher. We will get talking about all those rules and laws the exspurts down in Lansing and Washington pass that are totally unreal, and my buddy will say, "Always remember that an ex-spurt is only a drip under pressure!" Now, I wonder.....

But then, you have all these TV shows on with an outdoor Exspurt on just about everything. Let's be real now. Do they ever get skunked out there fishing? Do you ever see them spending all day baiting hooks for the kids and getting the kids' lines untangled? Or get the boat unloaded and the motor won't start? Somehow, someway, I get the feeling these exspurts have never hunted or fished out there in the real world.

Let me give you an example of an Exspurt. One night I happened to be going through the cable channels and came across this Exspurt fisherman who had his own TV show. It happened that on this show he was fishing an area off Lake Superior that I was in charge of, so I decided to watch this show. Here is our Exspurt telling people how it should be done and where the nice steelhead fishing is in the U.P. As I watched, I couldn't believe it. So I got on the phone and called a Conservation Officer that worked for me and worked the area in the program. I told him, "John, you blew it and missed one. "He replied, "You must be watching the same program I'm watching." Then we both had a good laugh. Why? Because here was this Exspurt going along a trout stream running out of Lake Superior with an illegal device used to take trout in the spring of the year in that area! I told John, "Maybe we ought to send him a ticket in the mail. We have what he's doing on film, and he is even telling us he's doing it."But you have to understand that this fishing Exspurt was a "troll"(a person that lives below the Big Mac Bridge.), and therefore, you get what you pay for. Now, remember what an Exspurt is, "A drip under pressure", and life will be a lot easier to understand.

Huskavarina edumacation: There has always been a feeling that there is more wisdom learned at the back end of a chain saw than you learn in college. The more some of us see and hear what is going on in our country, the more we have to wonder. It was always an amazement to those that worked out in the field for the government to see someone go off to the "Big House" on a promotion and forget everything they learned out in the field in the first six-months they were there! In fact, some of us always felt that about halfway down through the lower peninsula there was an invisible force field that made up a brain sucking machine, and by the time they passed through this going to the "Big House", they were useless to us living in the U.P.

We used to suggest that everyone after about a year or two down in Lansing's or Washington's "Big House" ought to have to spend six months back in the woods on the working end of a chain saw to get the feeling for how the real world lives again. That is why the U.P. is a special place, because from the woods, to the mines, to the papers mills, most of its people have a Huskavarina Edumacation.

Sometimes I think it makes them special people as you can see by some of my stories.

Bugs: Back when I was a kid, a bug was not an insect. It was something you rode in going hunting. (Look at the picture in the books of us hunting in the 40's and 50's, and you will see our Bug.) You would take an old Model T or A and put oversize tires on it to raise it up off the ground. Then you would find some old tire chains. Most of the time they had no body left on them, and you were to hang on for dear life when you came to a big mud hole. A party always had this saying, "It's hard to get two-tons stuck at fifty miles an hour, but when you do you are really stuck." I always said, "You are never stuck till you stop, so the key is never to stop till you hit high ground again." All the hunters used these vehicles back before anyone ever heard of a 4x4 pickup. They were homemade, and you were really someone when you had one. In fact I cannot count the times we gave the Game Warden a ride back into the backcountry when he had something to check on because he was not lucky enough to own a "Bug". But, now if a person was to make one and try to use it, they would end up having to hire a secretary to file the nine thousand-four hundred-seventy-five million tickets you would receive for having this dangerous vehicle back in the woods. Man, those were the good old days; No ORV laws, no snowmobile laws, about half the hunting laws, and no Big Mac bridge to let all those idealists across into God's country.

Yoopers: Have you ever been asked, "What's a Yooper?" It seems that there are certain terms that the real world has not used yet. If you take the Upper Peninsula of Michigan abbreviated, namely "The U.P. and sound it out what do you get? It has to be the word Yooper. Therefore all the good people (natives only) that make their homes in the U.P. of Michigan have to be Yooper. Right?

Up here in Yooper Country we have our own jokes, our own Yooper singing groups, our own terms, and a great life style.

The one thing that you want to remember is that you are born a True Yooper. It cannot be bought, you cannot get it by living here for years and years, and you must be born a Yooper. We have a real problem with Trolls (Those that live below the Big Mac Bridge.) coming up to Yooper land then trying to act like or become one of us, it just cannot be done! You either have it or you don't. You can come see us, we are glad when you spend your money here, we like you for a friend, but remember when you leave Yooper Land you leave as you came, not as a Yooper.

ORDER FORM: J.A.W.'S Publications
530 Alger Ave.
Manistique, MI 49854
(906) 341-2082

Name: _____

Address: _____

_____

1- *A Deer Gets Revenge* . . . . *$10.00 Postpaid*
2- *A Bucket of Bones* . . . . *sets only*
3- *From the Land Where BIG Fish Live* . . . . *$10.00 Postpaid*
4- *Luck, Skill, Stupidity* . . . . *$10.00 Postpaid*
5- *Humans are Nuts!* . . . . *$10.00 Postpaid*
6- *But! But! Honey It Wasn't My Fault!* . . . . *$10.00 Postpaid*
   Set of all six books $50.00 postpaid while they last. Any five books $40.00 postpaid.